For J and J, M and C and L and M,
S and W and M and J and P, B and
B and e, everyone at S, and
because SWF.

—Craig

Paula and Jonah, thank you for
putting up with me while I had my
head down.

—Andrew

Table of Contents

Chapter 3   Adaptive Images 59

Chapter 4   Understanding Media Queries 77

Chapter 5   Responsive Content 103

Chapter 6 Responsive Boilerplate 125

Preface

Your audience may never know about Responsive Web Design. What they will know is that your application either works on their device, or that it takes a lot of energy to make it work. Responsive Web Design is about ensuring the user enjoys the best experience possible when visiting your website. Primarily, that involves the minimum amount of resizing and scrolling while navigating your site, be it on a desktop machine, netbook, or smaller mobile device.

The techniques of Responsive Web Design enable your users to simply enjoy an optimal experience, and save you the hassle from having to create a unique user experience for each user and every device. RWD helps you deal with the very real problem of not knowing where and how your application will be used. Now is the time to embrace RWD.

Who Should Read This Book

Anyone involved in the Web, from business owners to agency designers, corporations to developers.

Conventions Used

You'll notice that we've used certain typographic and layout styles throughout this book to signify different types of information. Look out for the following items.

Code Samples

Code in this book will be displayed using a fixed-width font, like so:

```
<h1>A Perfect Summer's Day</h1>
<p>It was a lovely day for a walk in the park. The birds
were singing and the kids were all back at school.</p>
```

If the code is to be found in the book's code archive, the name of the file will appear at the top of the program listing, like this:

```
                                                    example.css
.footer {
  background-color: #CCC;
  border-top: 1px solid #333;
}
```

If only part of the file is displayed, this is indicated by the word *excerpt*:

```
                                           example.css (excerpt)

  border-top: 1px solid #333;
```

If additional code is to be inserted into an existing example, the new code will be displayed in bold:

```
function animate() {
  new_variable = "Hello";
}
```

Also, where existing code is required for context, rather than repeat all the code, a ⋮ will be displayed:

```
function animate() {
  ⋮
  return new_variable;
}
```

Some lines of code are intended to be entered on one line, but we've had to wrap them because of page constraints. A ➡ indicates a line break that exists for formatting purposes only, and should be ignored.

```
URL.open("http://www.sitepoint.com/responsive-web-design-real-user-
➡testing/?responsive1");
```

Tips, Notes, and Warnings

 ## Hey, You!

Tips will give you helpful little pointers.

Ahem, Excuse Me ...

Notes are useful asides that are related—but not critical—to the topic at hand. Think of them as extra tidbits of information.

Make Sure You Always ...

... pay attention to these important points.

Watch Out!

Warnings will highlight any gotchas that are likely to trip you up along the way.

Supplementary Materials

http://www.sitepoint.com/books/responsive1/
The book's website, containing links, updates, resources, and more.

http://www.sitepoint.com/books/responsive1/code.php
The downloadable code archive for this book.

http://www.sitepoint.com/forums/showthread.php?887181-Responsive-Web-Design
SitePoint's forums, for help on any tricky web problems.

books@sitepoint.com
Our email address, should you need to contact us for support, to report a problem, or for any other reason.

Do you want to keep learning?

Thanks for buying this book. We appreciate your support. Do you want to continue learning? You can now get unlimited access to courses and ALL SitePoint books at Learnable for one low price. Enroll now and start learning today! Join Learnable and you'll stay ahead of the newest technology trends: http://www.learnable.com.

Once you've mastered the principles of responsive web design, challenge yourself with our online quiz. Can you achieve a perfect score? Head on over to http://quizpoint.com/#categories/RESPONSIVE.

Acknowledgements

Craig Sharkie

This book wouldn't be what it is today without the guidance of the SitePoint team. The book's pace and rhythm was set by the team, and their style has capped off the whole process.

Above even these, though, is the team from Web Directions: http://webdirections.org. John Allsopp and Maxine Sherrin, along with Guy Leech and Lisa Miller, provide not only the excellent website that's inspired the examples in this book, but the series of technical events that inspire me each year.

Andrew Fisher

Typing words into as computer is easy; having them make sense is altogether more difficult. Thanks to Simon, Diana, and Kelly at SitePoint for their efforts to do so, anything that reads well is their doing more than mine. Craig not only wrote most of the book but also reviewed my contributions, so I want to thank him for the great feedback and for creating space for someone else to contribute.

Becoming Responsive

The longer you spend working with the Web, the more you come to realize the truth in the adage that change is the only constant. We've seen changes in our programming languages, design patterns, and browser popularity; more recently, the devices that connect to the Web and our applications have evolved. And it's this last change that has caused the need for **Responsive Web Design (RWD)**—an approach to web design that places the user firmly as the focus.

Changes in devices aren't new, of course; it's the pace and breadth of the change that's new. It was only a short time ago that our biggest challenge was whether our sites should make what seemed the giant leap from 800px to 1024px wide. Making the change, we thought we'd bought ourselves some time and that technology shifts would be slow, but technology knew better. As monitors and screens continued to grow, our challenge was in deciding how much of the full screen we should design for as devices also increased in pixel resolution. And higher pixel counts are not restricted to larger screens either; the rise of mobile devices means that screens are also shrinking.

You now have mobiles in portrait and landscape mode, tablets in portrait and landscape mode, laptops, desktops, monitors, and even televisions to contend with.

What we needed was an approach that allowed us to have our designs respond to any device they found themselves on, such as those shown in Figure 1.1, which is just the tip of the iceberg. And so responsive web design was born.

Figure 1.1. Viewing sitepoint.com across the tip of the iceberg

In addition to changes in the device sizes that applications can appear on, there are also changes to *how* users interact with your applications. The interface between the user and the application is becoming more invisible, more natural. While accessibility experts were rallying for better keyboard and mouse support, your application now has to contend with touch and gesture events, and game controllers as input devices. More recently, the rise of Apple's Siri and changes to Google TV mean that voice control is no longer the stuff of science fiction.

Responsive web design is a series of techniques and technologies that are combined to make delivering a single application across a range of devices as practical as possible. And it's not just web professionals who have seen the need; large and small businesses are seeking ways to make their web content work, regardless of where a user might encounter it.

Write Once and Run

Ethan Marcotte, credited as the father of RWD, published an article on *A List Apart* in May 2010 that he cunningly titled "Responsive Web Design."[1] In it, he focused on fluid grids, flexible images, and media queries as the technical pillars for RWD.

---

[1] http://www.alistapart.com/articles/responsive-web-design/

Marcotte also determined the need for a new approach to content to match those foundations.

The aim of these pillars was to achieve the elusive "write once, run anywhere" goal. By embracing RWD, with the content-driven changes it has brought about, we can rely on our applications adapting to a user's device choice. Rather than focus on devices, we focus on our users.

A veteran developer, Marcotte had spent years researching and advocating the techniques in his article. Because these techniques are based on long-standing, best-practice development principles, the barriers to entry are much reduced, with many designers already including elements of RWD in their work without realizing it.

It also means that even small changes in how applications are delivered can have sweeping changes for your users, and often such changes help future-proof your work. With the rapid growth of mobile devices, the scale of new devices can mean your applications become less usable. Although users have learned through necessity to double-tap the screen to zoom in, RWD can avoid this and help improve the user experience.

A simple change creates a better default experience for those with smaller and variable screen resolutions. Simply adding a `viewport meta` element can adapt your site—provided you have the right attributes—to mobile- and tablet-display sizes.

We'll look more closely at the possibilities this element offers later in the chapter, but, in the meantime, Figure 1.2 gives a nice insight. In the browser on the left-hand side, the UI loads as we've come to expect from old-school desktop sites in a mobile browser. On the right-hand side, the UI loads at a more usable scale. You'll need more than just this one change, obviously, but it should whet your appetite for what lies ahead.

Figure 1.2. Applying viewport properties to SitePoint's website

But there's still room for improvement. Figure 1.3 shows the same website on an iPad, using Safari in the first two shots, and Chrome in the third. The first shot has no viewport set and the other two have the same setting, but notice how Chrome just fits better? There are still some kinks in the tools we have, but RWD is growing stronger and it's just getting started. And how could you stop there? With fluid grids, flexible images, and media queries at our disposal, our arsenal is almost fully stocked.

Figure 1.3. iPad Safari without viewport, with viewport, and Chrome with viewport

The Pillars of Responsive Design

The next four chapters will look at each of the pillars of responsive design: fluid grids, flexible images, media queries, and dynamic content. Let's start with the big picture.

Fluid grids, the first pillar of RWD, are the natural successor to the fluid layouts that were hot topics in 2006 when the 800-to-1024 discussion was on the table.[2] Fluid typography plays a role here too, as your content needs to be as responsive as your layout.

Laying the Web out in grids and columns has been the dream of designers since the Web began. Implementations are yet to make it through, but the tide could be turning with advances being made by the W3C in setting standards. As there are no specific columns or grids in HTML—even in HTML5—we need to use the tools at hand. Frameworks are the most popular solution to quickly apply the structure of a grid, such as the 960.gs[3] framework seen in Figure 1.4.

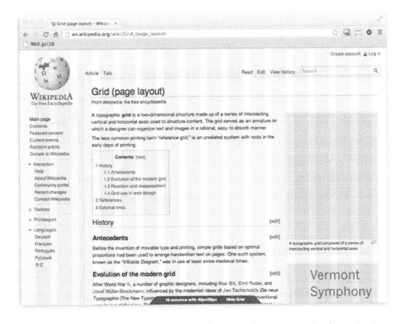

Figure 1.4. Wikipedia's Grid entry overlaid with the 960 Grid System, 16-column structure

---

[2] http://www.cameronmoll.com/archives/001220.html
[3] http://960.gs

Speed of development is just one benefit to using frameworks; the HTML and CSS we rely on is cross-browser and backwards-compatible, extensible, and accessible to a broad range of developers. When the W3C's solution is supported in browsers, it will provide us with power and flexibility; until that time, the libraries and tool sets we'll look at in Chapter 2 bridge the gap solidly.

The second pillar, flexible images (or adaptive images as it's called in the HTML5 specification), look to solve two problems: the difficulties in predicting the dimensions at which an image will display, and the resolution at which images can display. To meet these challenges, adaptive image techniques range from ways to allow your site's images to better accommodate fluid grids and layouts, all the way through to new proposals in HTML5 that would see different image sources used by different devices. How you combine these techniques for the best results will come down to a balance between your abilities and your users' expectations, and we'll help you with that balance in Chapter 3.

The difficulty with images is that where grids are structural, an image's quality and efficiency are more obvious to your users. Your users will probably fail to notice that you're even using a grid—they'll just enjoy the benefits—but they're likely to perceive stretched, pixelated, or undersized images.

Many manufacturers are also changing the pixel density that devices can show, resulting in 1.5 to 2 times the number of pixels showing across a range of devices. If your application fails to make use of that density, it can leave your users feeling shortchanged. Conversely, if your application only uses high-density imagery, and your users predominantly use your applications on older mobile devices or desktops, they'll be downloading images their devices are unable to exploit. That's wasted bandwidth for both you and your users, not to mention the wasted effort on the part of your team.

Figure 1.5 builds on the resolution example images from HTML5 Rocks.[4] The baboon on the left is showing at the 100×100px called for in the layout. On the right is the 200×200px image that will be delivered to devices that support high density display. In the middle is the resulting super-sharp version of the 200×200px image displayed at the specified 100×100px.

---

[4] http://www.html5rocks.com/en/mobile/high-dpi/

Figure 1.5. HTML5 Rocks image resolution baboons

Marcotte's last technical pillar was media queries. These bear the honor of being the strongest HTML5 contender in the mix, and also having the best cross-browser support. They might not work natively in older Internet Explorer versions—well, anything before IE9—but the shims to augment older browsers are solid and accepted.

Media queries work with the devices and browsers your applications find themselves on, and allow your application to respond to those devices, as seen in Figure 1.6.

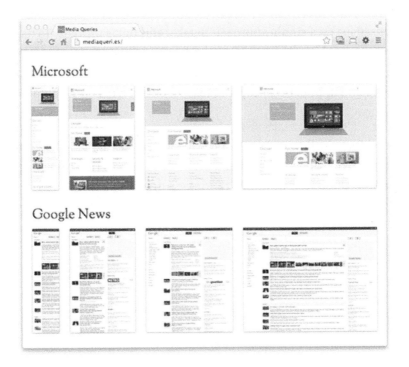

Figure 1.6. mediaqueri.es entries for Microsoft and Google News across devices

Device features are used by the media queries that can, in turn, direct which CSS is applied to your application. Media queries assess the capability of a device; for instance, is the browser capable of meeting these requirements? If so, then load this CSS or execute these rules:

```
<link rel="stylesheet" media="print" href="print.css">
<link rel="stylesheet" media="projection and (color)"
  href="projection.css">
```

As the media queries syntax is based on media types that have been around since CSS2.0 (1998, with a major revision in 2008), their basics should be quite familiar.

The first example above is a media type, the second a media query. If it weren't for the fact that the second `link` had an expression in the value of the `media` attribute, rather than a comma-separated list of types, the two elements are identical. We'll explore more of that strength and the power of media queries in Chapter 4.

Our last pillar is dynamic content, and we look at this in Chapter 5. Dynamic content is the newest addition to responsive web design and is still in flux. RWD adherents agree that a content strategy that places the user at the center is needed, but there's yet to be consensus on a single approach to take, and that's unlikely to happen. Just as RWD proposes technical solutions that adapt to a user's technology, it also tries to adapt to changes in the user's reliance on your content. As the interactions between users and applications become less visible, RWD will be able to take on more of the heavy lifting.

RWD suggests that a call to action changes priority once you've taken that action, or that a home page changes its content when there are changes to your physical location, as Web Directions South 2012[5] demonstrates in Figure 1.7.

---

[5] http://south12.webdirections.org

Figure 1.7. Web Directions South 2012 could show you the schedule when you arrive at the venue

So, there you have it. Responsive web design is the logical reaction design and developer communities are taking in the face of broad and disruptive upheaval from modern devices. The community is looking to establish a future-proof practice as well; they're looking ahead rather than just reacting to the devices on the market today. It sees RWD simply becoming the standard operating procedure. Once we've made the RWD transition, all applications will be built this way.

Refit or Restart

So we know that responsive web design is something that just makes life easier for our users. When, though, is the best time to start incorporating RWD in your process? Is it best to start from scratch when adopting an RWD approach? Is it best to leave your current application standing and apply RWD where needed? The short answer is that you're best moving forward with RWD firmly in your sights. How best to do that will be different for each developer, application, and site developed.

If your structure is solid, applying the fluid grid practices—which we'll discuss in Chapter 2—might well be possible. If your content is solid and your CMS is flexible enough, a new theme may be all you need to add Chapter 4's media queries. If your code is robust, surgically inserting dynamic images from Chapter 3 could be a walk in the park.

Your application might not even require all the pillars of RWD.

Alternatively, you might dramatically shorten your redevelopment time by creating a new multicolumn layout from the ground up. Your CSS performance may be markedly improved if you go back to square one and apply media queries from a clean stylesheet. And creating templates so that subdomains can serve targeted content might solve all your image delivery needs.

Or you might combine approaches. Perhaps an existing site can be the foundation for new, complementary solutions for more devices.

Avoid being daunted by the size of an existing application, and don't let it stop you from commencing an RWD refit. Similarly, refrain from throwing out your current application in an attempt to start fresh. What's important is to simply start.

Making an Example of Ourselves

The first five chapters of this book started life as a presentation at Web Directions South in 2012,[6] so it's only fitting that we use the website from that event as our sample site. It's already had some RWD techniques applied to it, so we'll travel back in time a little and strip that out for a clean slate.

We're only going to use a single page from the site—the Speakers & Sessions page,[7] as seen in Figure 1.8—but it will serve admirably as our showcase. We need to keep in mind while we're poking around that the site supported the conference success-fully; any issues we find must only be looked at in the context that the site *worked*. We're just going to make it work a little better.

Because the goal of RWD is to champion the user in our application, let's see what we might change to achieve this, starting with the code. In all sites, there are code choices that make sense at the time of development, but become questionable as technology evolves.

As the site's already using some responsive techniques, we're going to strip it back a little. By rolling it back to a non-responsive state, we can clear the decks.

---

[6] http://south12.webdirections.org/
[7] http://south12.webdirections.org/speakers-sessions

Figure 1.8. Speakers and sessions at Web Directions South, 2012

Here's the structure for a single speaker from our sample Speakers & Sessions page:

```
<section>
  <h3>
  <h3>
  <section>
    <img>
    <article>
      <p>
    <aside>
```

```
<section>
  <article>
    <p>
```

Let's add some of the typical content back to see it in situ:

```
                              chapter01/snippets/speaker_live.html (excerpt)
<section class="vcard session-info active">
  <h3 class="fn" id="responding-to-responsive-
    design">Craig Sharkie</h3>
  <h3>Responding to Responsive Design</h3>
  <section class="speaker">
    <img width="65" height="65" alt="Photo of Craig
      Sharkie" class="photo"
      src="http://static.webdirections.org/webdirections/images/spea
➥ker_c_sharkie.jpg">
    <article class="note">
      <p>Craig has been a regular at Web Directions
        South since before it was Web Directions
        South. He's moved from the audience, through
        moderation, and on to being a presenter.</p>
      <p>...</p>
    </article>
    <aside>
      <a class="nickname url" href="http://twitter.com/@twalve">@twa
➥lve</a>
    </aside>
  </section>
  <section class="session">
    <article>
      <p>No matter what you do, your design is going
        to be responsive. Even if your response is
        to ignore Responsive Design, that's still
        a response.</p>
      <p>...</p>
      <p>...</p>
      <p>...</p>
    </article>
  </section>
</section>
```

There is room for change here, but zealous discussions of HTML5 will fall short of advancing our user-centric drive; so while we'll update the code, we're just setting the groundwork. The HTML5 isn't part of the response, but it makes it easier for us to respond, and our page will be lighter in bandwidth and have a DOM structure that's easier to alter.

Structuring Our Content/Blocks

First off, we'll switch the containing element from a `section` to an `article`, as each speaker's entry could be easily syndicated from this page to one focusing solely on a single track; for example, all the design sessions on a design track page. An `article` is a great choice here as the speaker's blocks in our page would be, "in principle, independently distributable or reusable."[8] Our new structure emphasizes this, creating a standalone, ready-to-syndicate block. It means we can reserve the `section` element to hold the sections of our content—design, development, and so on. So let's keep it simple:

```
<article>
  <h1>
  <h2>
  <div>
    <figure>
      <img>
      <figcaption>
    <p>
  <div>
    <p>
```

We've taken some of the depth from the DOM, so we can now target our code with less reliance on classes. A simpler code structure means that we can streamline our CSS and deliver both code and CSS to the user more quickly. Before we look at our CSS, we'll add that sample content back in for emphasis:

chapter01/snippets/speaker_html5.html *(excerpt)*

```
<article class="vcard session-info active">
  <h1 class="fn" id="responding-to-responsive-
    design">Craig Sharkie</h1>
  <h2>Responding to Responsive Design</h2>
  <div class="speaker">
    <figure>
```

---

[8] http://dev.w3.org/html5/spec/single-page.html#the-article-element/

```
      <img alt="Photo of Craig Sharkie"
        src="http://static.webdirections.org/web
        directions/images/speaker_c_sharkie.jpg">
      <figurecaption>
        <a class="nickname url" href="http://twit
          ter.com/@twalve">@twalve</a>
      </figurecaption>
    </figure>
    <p>Craig has been a regular at Web Directions
      South since before it was Web Directions
      South. He's moved from the audience, through
      moderation, and on to being a presenter.</p>
    <p>...</p>
  </div>
  <div class="session">
    <p>No matter what you do, your design is going to
      be responsive. Even if your response is to
      ignore Responsive Design, that's still a
      response.</p>
    ⋮
    <p>...</p>
  </div>
</article>
```

Simplifying CSS

Next, let's look at our CSS. Simplifying CSS can be a great source for boosting performance, even if you're just removing unused styles.[9] Another way to keep your CSS lean is through using as few classes as possible. Stringing together classes in CSS produces the worst-performing selectors, so relying on single IDs and elements will make your application load and style more quickly—hence, happier users. Simplifying CSS becomes even more aligned to RWD when you minimize the use of hacks in your code. You can rest more confidently by employing CSS with the widest browser support possible. We'll explore browser support issues shortly, but till then, let's lightly touch on an old favorite:

---

[9] https://developers.google.com/speed/docs/best-practices/payload#RemoveUnusedCSS

chapter01/wds/03_html5/stylesheets/sheet.css *(excerpt)*

```css
.session-info.active {
  max-height: 1500px;
  overflow: hidden;
}
```

Internet Explorer 6 has probably dropped off your support matrix by now even if it still registers on your user's radar, so it's still advisable to avoid chaining selectors. IE6 will only recognize the last selector in a chain, and will apply max-height and overflow to anything with the active class, and not just session-info elements.

Switching from chained classes to a class in the environment of an ID heads toward object-oriented CSS. It also provides a nice performance boost by reducing the number of classes. It may not be a panacea, but we are creating a better user experience:

chapter01/wds/03_html5/stylesheets/sheet.css *(excerpt)*

```css
#content .active {
  max-height: 1500px;
  overflow: hidden;
}
```

Tweaking the Semantics

The last area we'll look is the content itself in a speaker block. When we look at the code we changed, there are two content signposts for us: a div holding our speaker content, and a div for our session content:

```html
<div class="speaker">
<div class="session">
```

When we relate that to what we see in Figure 1.9, our left column is about the speaker, the right, about the session. It's easy to see it in the code, but a lot harder to view it in a browser. Our users lack the benefit of seeing those descriptions in the classes, so they have to learn for themselves that the two columns on the desktop view hold separate content, and associate that with the columns having different widths and lengths.

Figure 1.9. A typical WDS12 speaker block

So, how does that column structure work for mobile viewing? The live site addresses this issue by changing to a single-column layout, seen in Figure 1.10, but there's still nothing to differentiate the content.

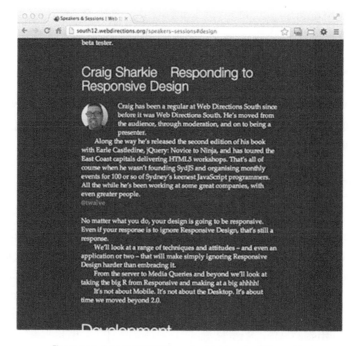

Figure 1.10. A typical WDS12 speaker block under 800px wide

With all the RWD work we do on the structural elements of our pages, keep in mind that tweaks to our content can be just as powerful. Changing the `font-size` of one column, changing the `font-family` of another, changing a column's `color`, or adding a heading to a column can assist users in discerning the two types of content.

Additionally, a thin version of our page, where the speakers' entries are only included in the code when they're required, can really decrease both page-load time and file size. As the WDS speaker entries start "closed," we could dynamically load the content to any of the speakers that catch our users' fancy. That way, they'll receive the great content they're interested in, instead of the heavy footprint it currently has. It's obvious the site is rich in content, but that mobile isn't the target device.

We'll be making more changes to our Speakers & Sessions in the coming chapters, but you can see that with a strong starting point, we can make plenty of inroads toward a responsive web design. Now we'll change our device target and look at the benefits of going back to the drawing board.

A First Look at Mobile-first Design

Despite the responsive web design movement being in its infancy, schools of thought are already forming around ways to change the basic approach. One of them is **mobile-first (MF)** design, which involves starting with an effective mobile site design and then augmenting it to produce the desktop version, rather that starting at the desktop and paring away unneeded components to support mobile devices. In the early days of RWD, there were few devices that demanded a mobile-centric approach, so there was little need to innovate in the space. As a result, the best and brightest were resolutely adapting from the desktop down. With the broadening range of mobile devices, though, designers are looking at MF in a new light, and as Andy Clarke said, "Oh, how we laughed when we realized our mistake."[10]

Shifting a design to MF focuses the discussion around content and interaction much earlier in the process, as it's almost impossible to "lipsum" (that is, fill the preliminary design of a website with lorem ipsum filler text) a mobile site. This focus on content helps shape and refine it in the mobile context (often seen as the hardest), which then flows out to all the other environments supported.

---

[10] http://stuffandnonsense.co.uk/projects/320andup/

Now there's nothing to say that if you choose to start your development from scratch, you must approach your design from mobile-first, but can you think of a better reason not to?

We've already discussed how our Web Directions South page has content that's not required for the first load. It's handy to remind ourselves that if our CSS has assets that have their `display` set to `none` for small devices, those assets are still downloaded. Not only would we be wasting potentially expensive data downloads on unused text, we'd be squandering even more bandwidth with undisplayed images. On top of that, there's the delay in page-loading time as unused assets are sourced. Media queries can help us out here, but if we were thinking "small screen first," we'd never have those unnecessary images to contend with in the first place!

Speaking of media queries brings up an interesting requirement for mobile-first designs. We covered how you may have dropped support for IE6, but there's a gotcha for Internet Explorer 7 and 8 when it comes to media queries—they don't work! There's no way to access these browsers on any mobile devices, but if you've gone mobile-first, you'll be delivering your site to desktops as well. If your site relies on queries to shift between its mobile and desktop views, IE7 and 8 will fail to switch views. This simply means that the conditional comments[11] you've used to deliver targeted styling solutions to IE might also become part of your RWD toolkit.

 Even JavaScript Can Only Do So Much

If you're relying on a JavaScript shim to deal with an older browser's lack of RWD support (for example, using Respond.js,[12] which used to come as a standard option in Modernizr[13] and 320 and Up), remember that it's impossible to guarantee that your users will have JavaScript enabled. Most will, sure, but some won't. And for any of your users with JavaScript turned off, the shim will have no effect, which is why you need to ensure that your design is strong enough to keep those users on the site—although it might just be 320px wide on the desktop.

Your hosting server's access logs should provide insight into your user's browser choices and take away some of the guesswork. It's likely you'll find that finance

---

[11] http://msdn.microsoft.com/en-us/library/ms537512(v=vs.85).aspx
[12] https://github.com/scottjehl/Respond/
[13] http://modernizr.com/

sectors in the UK and Australia tend to have older, locked-down browsers compared to creative industries in the US, for example.

Not only will your browser statistics allow you to make better decisions about the level of support you offer, it will show you when there's no value in the effort. You can avoid the "we have to support it because of this one person" type discussions.

Any Viewport in a Storm

Another staple that you'll want to look at before you finalize both a refit or restart approach is the use of the `viewport meta` element. In fact, whether you're building a responsive site, or a mobile-only site, you'll want this element:

```
<meta name="viewport" content="width=device-width,
  initial-scale=1.0">
```

Safari and Chrome on iOS devices and browsers on Android devices have the browser's viewport set at 980px wide. What's odd is that the device itself might only be 320px or 480px wide, depending on whether it's oriented in portrait or landscape.

This quirk means that your site looks two or three times smaller than you'd expect. Rather than natively showing the top-left third of your 960px-wide site, the browser shrinks everything down.

This can be useful if you've yet to make your site responsive, but can be painful if your application is targeted to the device width. Our `viewport meta` element will come to the rescue, though! `initial-scale=1.0` should need little explanation—the application first loads at a 1:1 ratio. The `width=device-width` only proves troublesome until you learn that the width before the equals sign is short for "viewport width." This attribute changes the viewport of the browser to the width of the device. Our targeted application fits like the proverbial!

```
<meta name="viewport" content="width=device-width,
  initial-scale=.43">
```

Don't feel that you're locked at 1.0 as your initial scale, though. Some great wins can be made with a little creative use of the viewport scaling. Take our SitePoint example from Figure 1.2. I changed the scale with some experimentation to 0.43

and the result returns the focus back on the user's experience, as you can see in
Figure 1.11.

Figure 1.11. Scaling new heights

If your users have to zoom your site every time they open it, why not meet them
halfway? For SitePoint, that 0.43 scale nicely coincides with the width of the main
content column on the site. The sidebar's just off to the right, the page's top navigation remains unchanged, and the logo receives a nice step up. All that, as well as
the primary content on the site—the reason your users visit—takes pride of place.

One word of warning as we move on from our `viewport meta` element—avoid adding
more controls than you need. If you're searching for scaling solutions online, be
aware that developers seeking to emulate native devices with their web application
often apply more stringent controls, creating usability issues for the unwary.[14]

If you were to deliver that 0.43 scale to an iPad tablet, for example, it would reduce
your usability rather than improve it, as evident in Figure 1.12.

---

[14] http://blog.javierusobiaga.com/stop-using-the-viewport-tag-until-you-know-ho/

Figure 1.12. Plumbing new lows

Reacting to the Responsive Movement

The tools and techniques that come under the banner of responsive web design have always been staples of the development community—and will continue to thrive as the practice of RWD breathes new life into them. The pillars of RWD provide a set of techniques that can be applied singularly or collectively to help position your users as the application's focus. The combination of fluid grids, dynamic images, media queries, and responsive content provide the opportunity to cater to the array of devices your application will feature on. Best of all, this is just the beginning ... bet you can't wait to see what lies ahead!

Fluid Grids

We know that while computer monitors and laptop screens grow wider—with more pixels displaying on them—mobile devices are popularizing the smaller dimensions on offer. More than ever, we need a design approach that caters to our growing range of screen widths, as depicted in Figure 2.1.

Figure 2.1. The SitePoint website across one laptop, two desktops, three iPhones, and four iPads

The Role of Fluid Grids

The fluid grids of responsive web design are part of this approach. On the Web (and off), a grid is a way to manage space in a layout, as shown in Figure 2.2. The simplest grids—made up of one, two, and three columns—typically have content that fits within a single horizontal row. More complex grids (having upwards of 9, 12, or more columns) also start to bring in higher row counts to control content. In complex grids, the vertical columns act more as registration points for laying out a row's content. In a 12-column grid, for example, a row might span all 12 columns, contain three regular spans at columns 1, 4, and 8, four spans at columns at 1, 3, 5, 8, or any combination.

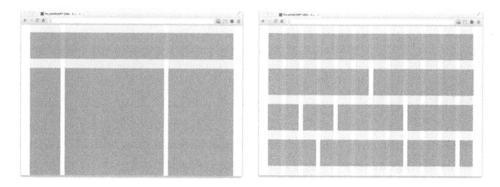

Figure 2.2. Simple versus complex grids

And while grids on the Web follow print grids in displaying with fixed widths, they also have the luxury of becoming fluid. Fluid grids have columns and gutters—the space between columns—where the widths are relative to their containers. The containers themselves can be either fixed width or relative, but the columns must be a proportion of their container to earn the fluid label, as expressed in Figure 2.3.

What an RWD fluid grid does best is provide a way to stop worrying about the grid, particularly in terms of how content on the page is laid out. Rather than setting the layout of your site in fixed-pixel widths, fluid grids use their proportional sizing to adapt to a user's device. Done right, we're able to concentrate on content and our user's experience, rather than the structure of our application.

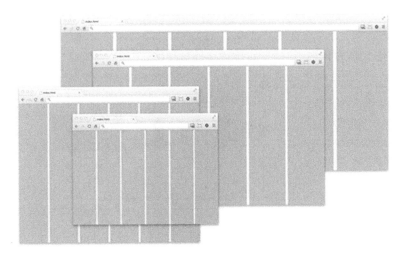

Figure 2.3. Fluid grids as a proportion of their container

In Figure 2.4, Microsoft's home page is displayed at 1440px and 1024px widths. At its widest, the three columns under the **For home** heading take up almost the same width as the entire site at the 1024px width, shown in Figure 2.5. The layout has expanded to fill more available space, and elements like columns, images, and gutters between columns have grown proportionally.

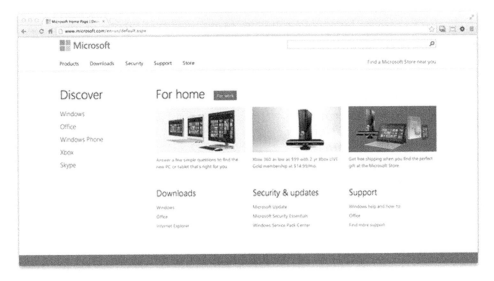

Figure 2.4. Microsoft site at 1440px wide

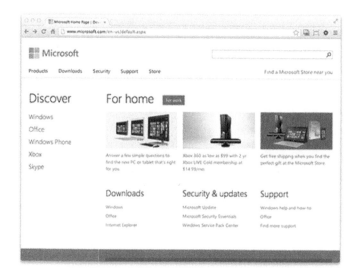

Figure 2.5. Microsoft site at 1024px wide

Once, the site would have been locked at 780px wide to fit comfortably on an 800px wide display with room for scrollbars. Now it takes up 95% of the screen width for most screen sizes. Simple! Rather than coming up with multiple designs to accommodate larger and smaller devices, the design moves fluidly depending on the browser size. Fluid grids take on the heavy lifting and leave you to focus on design instead of structure, so let's look at that structure now. We'll focus on those **For home** columns once more:

```
<section class="row-padded">
  <div class="grid-container">
    <div class="grid-row row-4">
      <div class="grid-unit col-3">
        <h2>For Home</h2>
        <div class="grid-row row-3 features">
          <div class="grid-unit">
          <div class="grid-unit">
          <div class="grid-unit">
```

The preceding code is a cleaned and smartly indented version of the code you'll find at microsoft.com. In it, the structure of the columns stand out, and the classes on the div elements make it even easier to read. We can focus on the class names alone, actually, and work our way back up our DOM. We start with three single grid-units wrapped in a grid-row. Then we work back up through the col-3, which creates the columns, and on to another `grid-row` with four children, because of the `row-4`, before we reach the parent `grid-container`. Then we finish at the `row-padded` element. We use `div` elements as there's no better HTML5 element for us. We simply need a structural element to apply our styling to, and obviously it's in the styling that the magic happens:

```css
.grid-container {
  width: 95%;
  margin-left: auto;
  margin-right: auto;
  max-width: 1180px;
}

.grid-row {
  clear: both;
  float: left;
  width: 100%;
}

.row-4 .col-3 {
  width: 74.5%;
  margin-left: 2%;
}

.row-4 .col-3 .grid-unit {
  width: 31.63%;
  margin-left: 2.555%;
  margin-right: 0;
}

.row-4 .col-3 .grid-unit:first-child {
  margin-left: 0;
}
```

As you can see, all the widths and margins being used are proportionally based on each element's parent. The three columns are roughly a third each of the available space; their parent—which is three columns out of the four in that row—is three-quarters of the row's width; the `grid-row` is the full width of its parent; the whole shebang is 95% of the viewport's width.

The Devil's in the Detail

The precision in the percentages (2.555% rather than 2.5) is to allow different rounding practices in browsers. Browser variation is nothing new to us, and it's the variations that make using the off-the-shelf grids at the end of this chapter so appealing. And while it might seem odd to pay so much attention to a column's possible rounding errors, remember that the final column in a 12-column grid has to cope with 11 columns' worth of rounding errors.[1]

A year before his RWD article on *A List Apart*, Marcotte published the cleverly named "Fluids Grids,"[2] where he pointed out that by using fluid grids "designers gain a rational, structured framework for organizing content and users gain well-organized, legible sites."

Using an off-the-shelf grid solution means that worrying about decimal places and cross-browser testing is unnecessary; you can push on with what you love doing: designing and developing great applications for your users. But before we decide which grid solution suits us best, we'll create a bespoke grid layout. We'll take a look at other great grid designers and their grid systems, and let them do the heavy lifting, but first we'll wrangle those decimals so that we know what we're getting into.

Monitoring the Growth

In the early 1980s, computer monitors' dimensions were a rather humble 320px by 200px, making the 800px by 600px resolution of the late 1990s seem impressive. Over the last five years, 1024 by 768 has become the norm, despite there being wider options available, and today the most popular monitors clock in at 1366 by 768. And they continue to grow, as is evident in Figure 2.6. Top-end consumer products are reaching 2560 by 1600, and Apple have introduced 2880 by 1800 with its Retina MacBook Pro.

---

[1] http://palantir.net/blog/responsive-design-s-dirty-little-secret
[2] http://www.alistapart.com/articles/fluidgrids

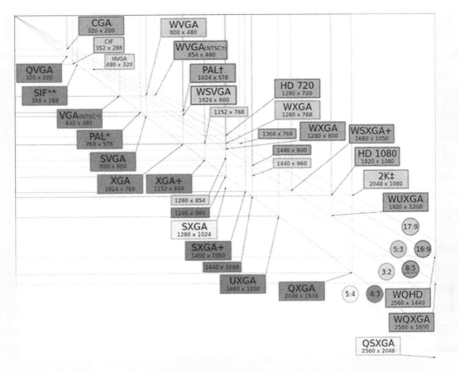

Figure 2.6. There are seven ratios across the 35 common screen resolutions

Creating Your Own Response

If you're starting from a clean slate, adopting a framework can offer a lot in terms of rapid prototyping and production-ready code. If you're dealing with an already published site, you may find creating a bespoke grid solution is more to your needs; you can better optimize the amount of code you deploy, and leverage code and styles already in your products.

That said, a tailor-made solution would need the same two features that mark the best frameworks: fluid grids with fluid typography. We'll start our exploration from typography and work from there. The characters in our type are the smallest atomic units on the page, so ensuring type is right will set the stage. There's actually a lot of shared solutions across the two features, and you'll find that when we've nailed one, we'll be well on the way to tackling the other.

Fluid Typography

Our goal here's to ensure that all facets of our typography are set in relative units. That way, all our typographic elements will flow and respond to changes in the devices that display our applications. Even more importantly, relative font sizing means that our users can influence our typography—they set the base size for our fonts and we scale from there. If we accept that a font's `font-size` should be relative and users should have the final say in the scale of their typography, but then restrict other typographic sizing to using fixed pixels, we're letting our users down and missing the opportunities of fluid typography. It's more than just about `font-size`; it's about the `padding`, `margin`, and `border` too.

Fonts being able to scale in a browser has been an issue since folks began talking about the need to scale fonts in a browser. Historically, the biggest problem with font scaling was the lifespan of one of the most successful browsers to date. Internet Explorer 6 rocketed Microsoft to more than a 90% share of the browser market, despite being unable to scale fonts described in pixels. It would have been less of a problem if the majority of sites at the time weren't describing font sizes in pixels.

In a bid to allow users to scale their fonts, developers and designers began to assign font sizing using relative measures in either percentages or ems (or, more recently, rems[3]). Even though IE6 is no longer the player it was, we'll build on the work of those pioneers of relative measures and take relative font setting to the next level.

The first point to take on board with fluid typography is that our users control it—we merely enhance from their base. Contrast levels, fonts, font sizes, and screen magnifiers are all adopted by visually impaired users, who set their own comfort levels. Even if our users are leaving the browser vendor's factory setting in place, they are still effectively setting their grade of comfort. To make our applications more accessible, we should steer clear of fixed-pixel sizing and work with relative sizing.

The ratios that those fixed pixel sizes give us will still be our goal, but we'll reach that goal using relative fonts. With fluid typography, our font ratios could be text at 1 unit, headings at 2 units, and margins at half a unit. We refrain from dictating the unit, but we trust our design. We make a conscious effort to *not* say our font

---

[3] http://css-tricks.com/snippets/css/less-mixin-for-rem-font-sizing/

size will be 12px, our main headings 24px, and that padding will be 6px. With RWD, establishing ratios between all your elements is the heart of the design process.

In Figure 2.7, the text on the left has a margin—the dotted area—with a fixed size of 6px. When the size doubles, the margin stays fixed. The text on the right has a relative size, so when the text doubles in size, the relative margin also doubles and maintains our design's proportions.

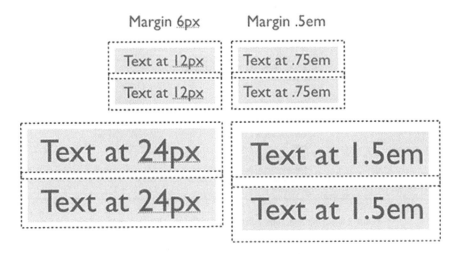

Figure 2.7. Relative margins maintain a design's proportions

Unmasking Default Font Sizing

Have a quick look round. Is anyone who makes browsers watching? We're about to make a point that seems to have escaped their attention. We're alone? Good …

All browsers in the market today have a default font size of 16 pixels.

There. I said it.

I can't find a reference as to *why* all browsers share this default `font-size` in their browser style sheets, but they do. It's one of the great mysteries of the Internet—one of those very rare cases where all browsers are in accord, and in accord without there even being a specification. We can draw lines back to the early Mosaic browser,[4] but then it's blank.

---

[4] http://www.ncsa.illinois.edu/Projects/mosaic.html

If you add a `font-size` of 100% to your `body` element and then view the computed size in your browser's developer tools area, you'll find that they all agree on 16 pixels, which we see in Figure 2.8.

chapter02/browsersheets/index.html (excerpt)

```
body {
  font-size: 100%;
}
```

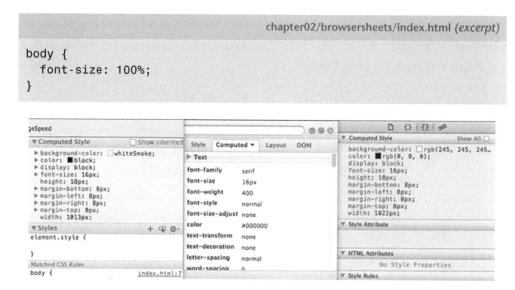

Figure 2.8. The default 16px `font-size` in Chrome, Firefox, and Safari

Wikipedia houses a great breakdown of the pixel's history,[5] but the most important factor for us is that we have a base font size across all browsers, and we can use this to make dealing with fonts a little easier. But with the goal of achieving easy-to-read, proportional font sizes, having a standard 16px font size will be no help to us. We need to return to what we're more comfortable with: a starting font size of 10px. To do that, we'll set our base `font-size` to 62.5% of the default 16px, which gives us a 10px base, and the happy effect that 1.2em would be 12px, 1.6em would be 16px, and so on. If you were at all concerned about using proportional fonts because of the weird numbers involved, we've just removed that barrier:

chapter02/relativelydifficult/index.html (excerpt)

```
html {
  font-size: 62.5%;
}
body {
  font-size: 1.0em;
```

---

[5] http://en.wikipedia.org/wiki/Point_(typography)

```
    ⋮
}
body > div {
  font-size: 1.2em;
    ⋮
}
```

Today, though, there's open acceptance of the 16px base, even a movement that holds that the 16px default should be once again embraced.[6]

The 62.5% technique takes much of the groundwork out of font sizing in a shallow DOM, or one where there's little change in font sizes from heading level to heading level. The downside is that while it makes relative sizes fairly easy to work with, it quickly unravels when we're changing the sizes of elements deep in our DOM. Drop the font-size in a sidebar, bump it up in the sidebar's article, and then try to calculate your h1 font-size. Figure 2.9 shows a common pitfall.

element	relative	computed
html	62.5%	16
body	100%	10
div#main	1.2em	12
section#content	1.6em	19
aside#sidebar	0.6em	12
article	1.0em	12
h1	2.0em	23

Figure 2.9. Chrome's interpretation of relative font sizing on child elements

Walking down the DOM, the html, body, and div are as we'd expect. The 1.6em we applied to the section failed to give us the 16px you might have expected, though, as its parent is 12px rather than 10px. Even more surprising is the 2em on the h1; its parent is 12px, but when you double it, the result is 23px—not 24px. Take a look at the example code with the book's source files and adjust the numbers to see if you can guess the results.

---

[6] http://www.smashingmagazine.com/2011/10/07/16-pixels-body-copy-anything-less-costly-mistake/

The example is still a very shallow DOM, and juggling the relative fonts remains an option here, but for deeper DOMs or legacy sites, it can quickly become tough. The temptation to head to the safety of pixels will be strong. We need a technique that has a far simpler formula for success.

Applying Relative Layout Units

If you change the scale at which you're viewing a site, and find that while the text responds and becomes larger, the distance between elements stays the same (or that elements start to crowd, or even overlap, each other) you can bet that the `font-size` is relative, but the `padding`, `margin`, or `line-height` (or even all three) is fixed-width and fails to respond to our user's needs. This is the case in Figure 2.10, so let's fix that.

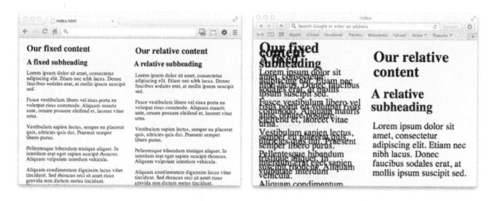

Figure 2.10. Fixed versus relative sizing where font size is doubled on the right

As we did in our 62.5% technique, we'll continue to work with a 10px font as our default, and we'll add to that element with 6px of padding; we'll also have headings that are double the font size but which maintain the same 6px padding. This time, though, we'll leave out the 62.5% change to the `html` element, and leave the base font untouched; we'll create our font in the context of our 16px starting point:

```
                              chapter02/relativelydifficult/index.html (excerpt)

body {
  font: normal 100% Helvetica, Arial, sans-serif;
}
```

We know that fonts inherit their base size from their parent element. Therefore, with the browser at its factory default, our target 12px is 75% of the starting default 16px size:

chapter02/relativelydifficult/index.html *(excerpt)*

```
p {
   font-size: 0.75em;
}
```

We also know that margins and paddings are relative to the element's font size, so for our initial calculations and with our p element's default font size of 12px, we know half an em will give us our goal of 6px. With our 16px default font size, we have the p element's target 12px font size and 6px of padding. Additionally, to match the 6px padding for our h1, we'll need to work out how 6px factors into 24px, the heading's font size; it comes in at a quarter of an em:

chapter02/relativelydifficult/index.html *(excerpt)*

```
p {
   font-size: 0.75em;
   padding: 0.5em;
}
h1 {
   font-size: 1.5em;
   padding: 0.25em;
}
```

What's important here is that we've set the ratios of those values, rather than the actual values themselves. If a visitor has set their base font to 36px, the ratios of the font sizes and paddings stay on target for our design; even better, we work with the user's settings. With a 36px base font size, for example, the p would have a font-size of 27px and padding of 13.5px.

There's no real need to know what the final calculated size is going to be as our user can change this at any time; however, we're aware it will fit the formula shown in Equation 2.1:

target ÷ context = result   (2.1)

The target is the element we're working with, the context is the DOM location our target is in, and the result is what we apply in our stylesheet. We take the font size we want and divide it by the font size we find ourselves in, and it gives us our result. You'll find this formula in Marcotte's "Fluid Grid" article on *A List Apart*,[7] and he might well have found it in Jon Tan's earlier article.[8] You'll also find it invaluable:

```
target / context = result
12 / 16 = 0.75
```

We plug that 0.75 straight into our CSS:

```
p {
  font-size: 0.75em;
}
```

We're on a roll, and we're going to stay proportional for the line-height property, too. We'll need a proportional unit, and as line-height has its own special proportional unit, we'll use that.

An element's line-height is inherited from the closest parent element in the DOM that has the line-height property set, and can be given a height in either a percentage, a fixed pixel height, or with two keywords: normal and number. Using either percentages or pixels can give some unusual results, unless you set and reset the line-height. Without resetting, percentages and pixels in line-height remain the same once set, irrespective of the element's font-size.

If we use the special unit normal or a unit-less number for our proportional value, CSS gives us the types of values we're after. The difference between the two options here is that normal is a "reasonable" number that changes with the font, browser, and platform.[9] In contrast, a number can be anything we set. We're in control! And since Web Content Accessibility Guidelines 2.0 (WCAG 2.0) recommend a line-height of 1.5 to achieve its top rating, we're going to go with that option.

We simply set a line-height of 1.5 on the body element, and it flows through all the elements on our page:

---

[7] http://alistapart.com/article/fluidgrids

[8] http://v1.jontangerine.com/silo/css/pixels-to-ems/

[9] http://www.w3.org/TR/CSS21/visudet.html#propdef-line-height

```
body {
  font: normal 100% Helvetica, Arial, sans-serif; /* 16px */
  line-height: 1.5;
}
p {
  font-size: 0.75em; /* 12px */
  padding: 0.5em; /* 6px */
}
```

Using number, we effect an accessible solution and the value just feels right in our CSS. We gain a proportional response for our line heights, and are able to apply the same control as when we select the contents of our font stack:

```
p {
  font: normal inherit 400 1em/1.5 Helvetica, Arial, sans-serif;
}
```

The simple formula (target ÷ context = result) we used for generating relative font sizes is going to come to our rescue once more with our fluid grid solution.

Handcrafting a Fluid Grid

As we did with fluid typography, we need to accept that the way users view our web applications is beyond our control. All we can hope to control is how we respond to what they're using to view our application.

When fluid layouts were first touted as the Holy Grail,[10] the push was to only ever allow sites built with 800px in mind to flow to the heady widths of 1024px. Rather than wedging a hundred pixels of whitespace each side of your design, you were encouraged to open the layout and enable it to flow to the full width. And it worked. But then displays expanded again, and the definition of "worked" had to change.

Luckily, when displays went wider, people stopped feeling the need to go full screen with their browser window. Even at their widest, there is still the possibility that windows won't be maximized, so we can wrap our layouts in some of that whitespace.

---

[10] http://www.alistapart.com/articles/holygrail/

Adding a Golden Ratio

Let's look at a column solution that, like our fluid typography, is designed to meet whatever display our users prefer. Our goal will be a two-column layout that we can be fairly certain will stand up to the rigors of modern desktops. We'll look at adapting our Speaker & Sessions layout for mobile and tablet displays in future chapters, but for now, two columns on a desktop display is our goal. We might even go crazy in the next chapter and go to a one-column layout, but that's only going to be possible if the foundations are right here.

Our first task is to establish the relative widths of our columns. We could plump for 50% of the total width for each column, or perhaps thirds. Instead, we're going to draw our inspiration from before 300 BC, when an Ancient Greek named Euclid wrote about the golden ratio: "a straight line is said to have been cut in extreme and mean ratio when, as the whole line is to the greater segment, so is the greater to the less." Or, more simply: a + b is to a, as a is to b, as demonstrated in Figure 2.11.

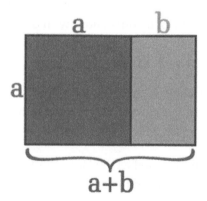

Figure 2.11. Euclid's golden ratio

In Figure 2.12, the left layout is how the two columns of the Speaker description look on the WDS site. On the right is our goal layout with its classic proportions.

Figure 2.12. WDS session information: left, in situ; right, golden ratio

From the columns of Ancient Greece's Parthenon to the spirals of sunflower seeds in nature, and on to medieval manuscript design, the golden ratio has featured in design for centuries. Human beings simply find the ratio's proportions pleasing. Even if this description is unfamiliar to you, its effect in design and nature will be well-known, like the nautilus shell from Figure 2.13.

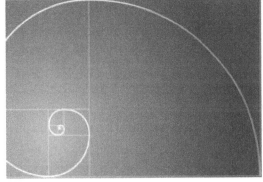

Figure 2.13. The golden ratio in nature and design

If you're keen, there's a lot more math you can take on board,[11] but the important points for us are the golden ratio's value: 1.6180339887, and its conjugate: 0.6180339887. We're interested in the conjugate because our formula uses the short length, the a, divided by the long, the a + b:

```
target ÷ context = result
   (a) ÷ (a + b) = 0.6180339887
```

---

[11] http://en.wikipedia.org/wiki/Golden_ratio

For an example of the formula at work, we'll use a standard 960px screen width and perform a little algebra. If we were only looking to create a fixed pixel-width layout, the result would be our wider column width:

```
target ÷ 960 = 0.6180339887
target = 0.6180339887 * 960
target = 593.312629152
```

The next step for a fixed pixel-width layout would be to find the smaller column width and do the same two calculations for every device width we were looking to deploy our application across. Sure, we would be happy to have found column proportions that have pleased designers for two thousand years, but that's a lot of work and we'd need to keep checking to make sure no new device widths were released. We have to return to an RWD solution.

960: The Poster Child for Factors

When grid designers look for a base width, they want as many factors as possible to give the greatest number of columns. 960 is divisible by 1, 2, 3, 4, 5, 6, 8, 10, 12, 15, 16, 20, 24, 30, 32, 40, 48, 60, 64, 80, 96, 120, 160, 192, 240, 320, 480, and, of course, 960.

Our formula has again made it easy for us to calculate responsive relative values, and it's gone one step further and verified our golden ratio percentages. Rather than setting our column width to 593px, we just use the percentage to set our width. Then, no matter what the page width, we'll have our golden ratio. So our larger column is 61.80339887%, leaving 38.1966012% for our second column. To make our layout more practical and robust, we'll add a gutter between our columns by subtracting 1% from both columns:

```css
#column-a {
  float: left;
  width: 60.80339887%;
}

#column-b {
  float: right;
  width: 37.1966012%;
}
```

We now have the foundation to start our own fluid grid solution using a fluid golden-ratio grid. This forms a solid basis for our explorations of media queries and beyond.

Off-the-shelf Grid Solutions

Off-the-shelf solutions take the goal of trouble-free structure to new heights. As well as relying on a fluid grid to focus on your application's experience, you're depending on another person's grid. All you need to do is find a solution you're comfortable with, sit back, and relax.

A quick search will soon show you more grid solutions than you can poke a stick at. A quartet of standouts you'll see mentioned again and again are 960 Grids,[12] Bootstrap,[13] Gridset,[14] and the innovative 320 and Up.[15]

Let's take a flying look at each of these, and then apply one of them to our Speakers & Sessions page. And while we're looking, keep in mind that you may not end up using any one solution from here, but there's aspects in each one that can help you in the long run. We'll look at the pros and cons, and shine a spotlight on a feature of each framework.

960 Grid System

Nathan Smith's 960 Grid System, seen in Figure 2.14, started life as unashamedly desktop-focused—perfect if you're looking for a desktop solution. For a mobile-first approach, Smith has more recently put in the hard yards to move the framework there too. To satisfy both approaches, 960 Grid System provides a raft of tools that include CSS and JavaScript files for rapid prototyping and publishing, as well as templates for many popular design environments such as Balsamiq, Fireworks, Omnigraffle, and Photoshop.[16] There are currently fifteen in total that ease the flow between design, development, and publishing.

---

[12] http://960.gs/

[13] http://twitter.github.com/bootstrap/

[14] https://gridsetapp.com/

[15] http://stuffandnonsense.co.uk/projects/320andup/

[16] https://github.com/nathansmith/960-Grid-System/tree/master/templates/

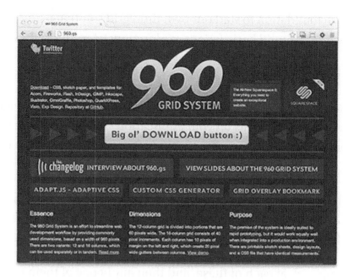

Figure 2.14. The 960 Grid System website

960.gs's attention to detail has seen it inspire elastic and fluid variations, themes, and even a system that lets you adapt your own CSS preferences.[17] Together, these mean you can set your preferred column number, column width, and gutter width—all while enjoying the benefit of the 960.gs community.

Pros:

- features custom CSS generator
- spawned other 960-based solutions, which ease its integration
- has a lot of divisors—28 all up—so a lot of column configurations

Cons:

- extra markup compared to a bespoke solution
- extra CSS file size compared to a bespoke solution
- nonsemantic class names

Spotlight

As some of your "users" will likely be bots from search engines, 960 Grid System also caters to these. It has a source order feature, which means you can have more

---

[17] http://grids.heroku.com/

important content higher in your DOM, but use CSS to have it appear where required in your page:

```
<h1 class="grid_4 push_4">960 Grid System</h1>
<p class="grid_4 pull_4">...</p>
```

The push_X and pull_X classes push and pull relatively positioned elements along their row in your grid. The 960 Grid System logo in Figure 2.14, for example, appears higher in the source order than the text block to its left, yet takes pride of place in the center of the UI.

Bootstrap

If you're on the Web today, you'll have heard of Twitter and GitHub, so when you hear of a framework that started life at Twitter is the most popular repository on GitHub—beating even jQuery and Node.js—you'll gain some idea of the viral spread that has engulfed Bootstrap, seen in Figure 2.15. In its own words,[18] it's a "sleek, intuitive, and powerful front-end framework for faster and easier web development." In short, it epitomizes the drive behind responsive web design to enable developers to quickly release applications that hold the user's needs at the forefront.

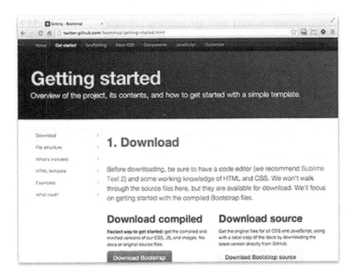

Figure 2.15. The Bootstrap website

---

[18] https://github.com/twitter/bootstrap

Bootstrap is best known for its component library, but its responsive features are strong enough to stand alone. We'll use Bootstrap to transform our Speakers & Sessions page shortly, where we'll exploit the fluid nesting and offsetting that help to set the framework above its peers. And while we'll avoid taking advantage of the component styling for which many developers adopt Bootstrap, the ease with which the grid comes to life will make you keen to explore the framework's other features.

You may even be tempted to utilize the growing community marketplace that's formed around theming Bootstrap. You can take a dip in the free themes from Bootswatch[19] and work your way up to a paid theme from WrapBootstrap.[20]

If you don't use one of the themes you find, you could take a leaf out of 320 and Up's book and employ Bootstrap-friendly classes in your own work. You might skip integrating now, but the classes are extremely solid and the framework is providing inspiration as well as a high benchmark.

Pros:

- popularity means the community is strong and developers are familiar with it
- has been extensively tested and survived critical scrutiny
- is fully customizable to include only features you want
- features a marketplace to sell and purchase UI skins
- it can "help nerds do awesome stuff on the Web"[21]

Cons:

- extra markup compared to a bespoke solution
- extra CSS file size compared to a bespoke solution
- nonsemantic class names

Spotlight

Bootstrap easily allows for nested columns and loses none of its responsiveness when it does. Based on a 12-column grid, you can nest as deeply as you choose, but you should ensure that each nested group has columns with Bootstrap classes that total 12. In the example following, two six-unit columns are the children of one

---

[19] http://bootswatch.com/
[20] https://wrapbootstrap.com/
[21] http://twitter.github.com/bootstrap/

column, and that column and its sibling are the children of a single 12-unit column. Each six-unit column has a width of 48.93617021276595%, and a left margin of either 2.127659574468085% or 0% for the first child. Combine those width and margin percentages and you have 100%:

```
<div class="row-fluid">
  <div class="span12">Fluid 12
    <div class="row-fluid">
      <div class="span6">Fluid 6
        <div class="row-fluid">
          <div class="span6">Fluid 6</div>
          <div class="span6">Fluid 6</div>
        </div>
      </div>
      <div class="span6">Fluid 6</div>
    </div>
  </div>
</div>
```

Bootstrap's done the number crunching and testing (as seen in http://twitter.github.com/bootstrap/assets/css/bootstrap.css), so you can focus on the design:

```
.row-fluid [class*="span"] {
  ⋮
  margin-left: 2.127659574468085%;
}

.row-fluid [class*="span"]:first-child {
  margin-left: 0;
}

.row-fluid .span6 {
  width: 48.93617021276595%;
  ⋮
}
```

Gridset

Gridset, seen in Figure 2.16, has the rapid prototyping and design focus that you expect from a class-leading framework. It provides you with easy-to-use tools so that you can put away your calculator when managing columns. It even has Mark

Boulton at the helm.[22] But can it allow you to collaborate with distant colleagues in real-time? Why, yes, it can!

Figure 2.16. Gridset

You can collaborate with your team around one laptop, or with your team around the world. Gridset is not about simply adding breakpoints to your CSS; it's about designing in the browser while looking outside it for inspiration.

Pros:

- able to easily set and compare multiple grids for different breakpoints
- can share your grids in real time
- its keyboard command can invoke an overlay showing your grid over your site
- you can add columns, alter ratios, change gutters, and never worry about the math

Cons:

- extra markup compared to a bespoke solution
- extra CSS file size compared to a bespoke solution
- nonsemantic class names

---

[22] http://www.markboulton.co.uk/

Spotlight

Gridset's WYSIWYG interface is as easy to use as dragging guides in Photoshop. You can drag columns to form irregular sizes, and the base grid becomes more flexible, as you can see in Figure 2.17. No need to force two regular unit columns into a double column; it just does it. Then you can combine and nest grids for a trustworthy asymmetric grid.

Figure 2.17. The blue column has been dragged to a custom width

320 and Up

320 and Up was the first high-profile responsive web design solution that addressed Mobile First design. Mobile First works from the basis that the common elements on both mobile and desktop versions of an application all exist on the mobile version. You design for the mobile device first, and then use progressive enhancement to augment the experience of the application on larger viewports.[23] You don't have to just focus on the framework's 320px base; it also provides breakpoints via media queries at 480px, 600px, 768px, 992px, and 1382px. Check it: Figure 2.18.

---

[23] http://en.wikipedia.org/wiki/Progressive_enhancement

Figure 2.18. 320 and Up

Pros:

- the download bandwidth for mobile devices is smaller so applications load faster
- able to separate the grid from the design "atmosphere," like typography and color
- version 2 removed the requirement for Respond.js
- has evolved from an extension to the HTML5 Boilerplate,[24] thereby standing on the shoulders of giants

Cons:

- extra markup compared to a bespoke solution
- extra CSS file size compared to a bespoke solution
- nonsemantic class names

Spotlight

320 and Up has no shim to force older, noncompliant browsers to cope with media queries that they don't support. Instead, rather than giving them extra JavaScript to load, 320 and Up's Andy Clarke recommends giving older browsers a stylesheet that includes a fixed-width container, so it can load less. Older browsers are unavailable on mobile devices, and are unlikely to be encountered on large-dimension,

---

[24] http://html5boilerplate.com/

high-end devices. As the owners of noncompliant browsers are used to fixed layouts, they'll appreciate the faster load of a 320 and Up site and won't miss a responsive design.

We Put the Cons in Consistency

We listed the same points of contention for each of our four frameworks: extra markup to create the grid, additional CSS to cover options in the grid, and nonsemantic class names in the grid. But while these points are often noted as negatives, smart coders will see them for the opportunities they offer.

Extra markup means that there's no need to juggle your own code to meet the framework's needs. Adding in their expected HTML can give you a better understanding of how the framework interacts with your application.

Extra CSS may have a larger footprint than bespoke CSS; however, it comes with the benefit of being able to quickly roll out new sections to your application, use an extra or fewer column in the new section, and rely on the CSS working across platforms and browsers.

As for nonsemantic class names where the framework's chosen class names (`span4`, `yui-b`, `grid_4`) won't be semantic in your site, they have a semantic value in the framework. `offset4` in the context of Bootstrap has a lot of meaning.

Pulling Up Our Bootstraps

Let's see what it will take to apply Bootstrap to our Speakers & Sessions sample page, shown in Figure 2.19. Keep up, because we'll be done quickly, and remember to take a look at the code archive[25] for this book to see the sample code growing.

---

[25] http://www.sitepoint.com/books/responsive1/code.php

Figure 2.19. Speakers & Sessions in the wild

The first step is to download the files we'll need after we've customized Bootstrap's components. The Bootstrap customize page[26] allows us to easily control which features to include, seen in Figure 2.20. Hit both the "**Toggle all**" buttons and you'll find one for **Choose components**—seen in Figure 2.20—and the other for **Select jQuery plugins**. We have no need for plugins for now, and we're only after the **Scaffolding** section's **Grid system**, so check that one on. Then scroll to the bottom of the page to the **Download** section and hit the **Customize and Download** button—you can't miss it, it'll be the giant blue button.

---

[26] http://twitter.github.com/bootstrap/customize.html

Figure 2.20. Bootstrap's elusive **Customize and Download** button

Now all you need to do is add the files from the downloaded ZIP to your application and reference the files in your `head` element:

```
<link rel=stylesheet
  href=frameworks/bootstrap/css/bootstrap.min.css>
```

Next, we'll go through our CSS and take out the 800px-width settings so that our flexible grid can work its magic. We want our block-level elements to completely fill the space allowed by their parent elements. We'll have the same level of control; we're just doing it with the environment and so saving us from extra CSS rules. We're commenting them out initially, but we could just as easily delete these declarations; as comments we can more easily track what our page was doing, as well as what it does after our changes. You'll end up with rules such as these:

chapter02/wds/04_grid/stylesheets/800.css *(excerpt)*

```
header {
    ⋮
/*  width: 800px; */
    ⋮
}

#content {
/*  width: 800px; */
    ⋮
}

#sponsors {
    ⋮
/*  width: 800px; */
}
```

With just this change in place, our page still looks quite good. Quite good until you open a Speaker entry, that is. With no maximum width on the content and the two columns floating to the left and right with fixed widths, we gain a ludicrously wide gutter between the columns, evident in Figure 2.21.

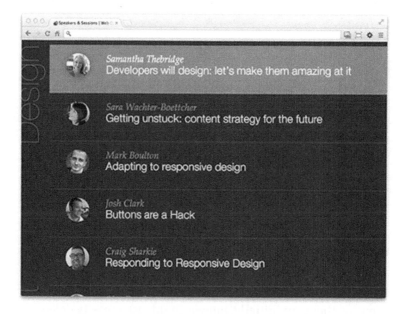

Figure 2.21. Speakers & Sessions without any width constraints

Let's fix that next. We'll try commenting out the content's widths in our stylesheet first:

chapter02/wds/04_grid/stylesheets/800.css *(excerpt)*

```
.session {
  /* width: 320px; */
}

.speaker {
  /* width: 240px; */
}

#content p {
  /* max-width: 480px; */
  text-indent: 2em;
}
```

We're going to go ahead and make the minimum number of changes and additions to our code and CSS to utilize the power of the framework. Without the constraints of widths, the CSS floats fail to work; they're next to go as they're unnecessary with Bootstrap. Then we'll add a little extra HTML. We need to wrap our columns in a div that we can add our row class to, and we'll add our column classes while we're there and justify our column's content—it will help show off our new columns:

chapter02/wds/05_bootstrap/stylesheets/grid.css *(excerpt)*

```
.session {
  /* float: right; */
  text-align: justify;
}

.speaker {
  /* float: left; */
  text-align: justify;
}
```

Our new Bootstrap classes introduce some interesting concepts. First and foremost is the goal of working in denominations of 12. Bootstrap uses a 12-column layout, so when we work within a row we try to make sure our elements classes add up to 12. As illustrated in Figure 2.22, it uses span4 + span6 + offset2, giving us our 12 units, so we know we're on track.

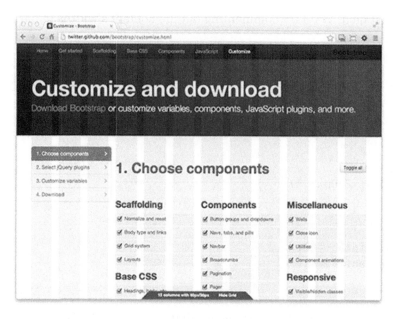

Figure 2.22. Bootstrap's page with its columns exposed

The second point is that there's no need to have 12 elements in a row, just 12 units, and we can reach our target using offsets. The `offset2` on our `session` div shifts the element two columns to the right of its position in the document flow. It's a powerful way to place your content without having to use empty holding elements in your UI:

```
<div class="row-fluid">
  <div class="speaker span4">
    ⋮
  </div>
  <div class="session span6 offset2">
    ⋮
  </div>
</div>
```

We're far from finished, sure, but we've only added a few classes, styles, and `div` elements and we're accomplishing great results. How much farther do we have to go? Let's take the `margin` out of our `article` elements so that our rows are the full width of our browser viewport, and then wrap all our content in a handy `div` with an `id` of `main` to set our breakpoint:

chapter02/wds/05_bootstrap/stylesheets/grid.css *(excerpt)*

```css
#main {
  margin: 0 auto;
  max-width: 1200px;
  width: 96%;
}
```

chapter02/wds/04_grid/index.html *(excerpt)*

```html
<div id="main">
  <header class="vevent">
    ⋮
  <section id="panel2" class="panel">
    ⋮
  <section class="content">
```

We've used a max-width of 1200px. It's a fairly arbitrary figure, but that's what Bootstrap considers the width of a large desktop device, and it allows us to show us what happens when the browser window is wider than our max-width. Bootstrap uses a 980px breakpoint as its "desktop" width, and 1200px as its "large desktop" breakpoint. Anything larger than 980px will stop Bootstrap from behaving fluidly; we want our content to flow, but we also want to stop that flow when the application's viewport is too wide to be easily read. And the 96% width ensures that there's a gutter around all the content, and allows for the original design having the Speaker content all the way out to the edges of their blocks.

Now we add another 12 column-unit offset and span to each of the Speaker blocks, and that'll just about wrap it up. offset1 means that the span11 actually starts in the second column, leaving us room for the section headings such as "Design" in Figure 2.23 to display properly:

```html
<article class="vcard session-info span11 offset1">
```

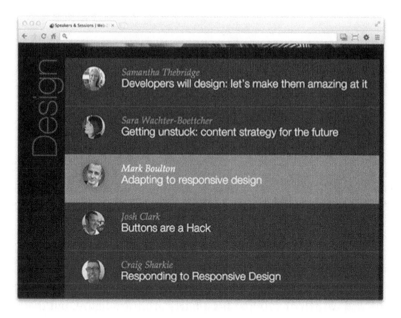

Figure 2.23. Speakers & Sessions with our comfortable any width gutter constraints

For our last step, we'll look at a regression that's crept in and apply an RWD approach to our JavaScript. The accordion feature that shows and hides the content of each Speaker's block will now be broken. The live script is checking for the presence of a fixed class name, `vcard session-info`, and as we're changing the `class` attribute value and adding Bootstrap classes on these elements, it will affect the JavaScript and the accordion fails to open. Rather than hard-coding `vcard session-info` in our JavaScript, we'll get the `className` value dynamically. Then, as we change class values in our testing, the accordion feature will just keep on working:

```
chapter02/wds/05_bootstrap/scripts/active.js (excerpt)

var sessions = document.getElementsByTagName("article"),
  length = sessions.length,
  className = sessions[0].className;
  ⋮
for (var i = 0; i < length; i += 1) {
  if (sessions[i].className === className) {
    ⋮
```

We have no way of knowing what the class actually is, but there's no need to—just like we're unaware which devices our users are using to view the site. Sure, that piece of JavaScript isn't strictly responsive web design, but the attitude of providing a flexible, extensible solution up front sure as heck is.

Our grab in Figure 2.24 shows the browser set to 1440px in width.

Figure 2.24. Speakers & Sessions breakpoints with Bootstrap applied: 1440px

Figure 2.25 shows the browser at 800px in width.

Figure 2.25. Bootstrap breakpoints at 800px

We can see that while the columns change width based on the browser, we still maintain integrity even at our widest view. The design of the sample pages might need some work to come up to scratch, but the Bootstrap fluid grid is working seamlessly.

Fluid Solutions

We've seen how fluid grids offer great flexibility and provide useful bonuses to development such as speed in deploying, testing, and maintaining code. If you employ a framework, you can now hire team members based on their knowledge of the framework you use. If you build your own solution and simply use the tried-and-tested frameworks as inspiration for your code, new team members will benefit from that inspiration. You can quickly roll out the structure of your applications and focus more of your efforts on designing the experiences that keep your users coming back. When we add the fire-and-forget benefits of using relative fluid typography in our fluid grids, our applications can respond to the devices they find themselves on—today and tomorrow.

Now we'll look to the next part of the solution, dynamic images, so that our graphics can have the same impact and responsiveness we've given our structure and typography.

Adaptive Images

Adaptive images, responsive web design's second pillar, allows us to provide image solutions with no restrictions to a fixed display size; adaptive images respond to different viewport sizes and display resolutions. It seeks to overcome two problems facing visual elements in the age of mobile development. Let's look at those now.

The first issue is that when a site's structure is fluid, its content must be just as fluid; otherwise, the structure will move and expose whitespace next to any inflexible content elements. And while fluidity is easy enough for a site's text, it's not so much the case for graphical elements. When you've labored over cropping an image to the exact size and shape you need, or compress it to just the right balance between quality and file size, you'll know that simply relying on a browser to adjust an image once it's live will be anything but trouble-free.

The second problem arises from the need to respond to the quality of displays on modern devices. Today's HiDPI (High Dots Per Inch) devices—the Retina display from Apple and its AMOLED siblings on Android devices—display up to twice as many pixels as we're used to, and with twice the pixels comes twice the resolution. A successful adaptive-images solution needs a mechanism for detecting the high Dots Per Inch (DPI) devices and delivering them the assets they deserve.

We need a way to address those two issues—asset size and asset resolution—in order to focus more of our attention on our users. Arguably, a single perfect solution eludes us, but before we're through we'll look at the problem of adaptive images from all angles—from CSS, through JavaScript, and on to HTML—and consider the pros and cons of each. Let's get the ball rolling again with a CSS solution.

Adaptive CSS

So far our CSS solutions have dealt with adapting our layouts, so let's see how CSS deals with our image-resolution challenge. There's no cross-browser solution for adaptive images in the CSS specification, so let's look at the leading experimental candidate, a proposal from Apple called image-set. image-set allows us to provide different background-image sources for devices based on pixel density. This results in a device being given an image that best utilizes its capabilities.

The image-set syntax relies on vendor prefixes to apply the value to supporting browsers. It wraps the url value from our CSS block and adds a modifier—in this case the 1x or 2x, but also 1.5x. This modifier responds to a device's pixel ratio and displays the image at its maximum ratio:

```
                                    chapter03/imageset/stylesheets/style.css (excerpt)

#set {
  background-image: url(../images/1_oppan.png);
  background-image: -webkit-image-set(
    url(../images/2_gangnam.png) 1x,
    url(../images/3_style.png) 2x
  );
  ⋮
  background-image: image-set(
    url(../images/2_gangnam.png) 1x,
    url(../images/3_style.png) 2x
  );
}
```

And it's not just the method and syntax that's experimental; image-set breaks new ground in applying the vendor prefix *after* the colon to the declaration value, rather than before the colon to the declaration property. Figure 3.1 shows the image-set declaration value displaying across a range of browsers: Chrome, Safari, Firefox, Opera, and Chrome on iOS. The WebKit-based browsers respond to the -webkit-vendor prefix showing the 2x image where possible, and on a non-Retina device they show the 1x image.

Figure 3.1. image-set on Chrome, Safari, Firefox, Opera, and Chrome on iOS

A device's pixel ratio is a way to describe the resolution of a screen measured in dots per pixel. Where dots per pixel have become tricky is when we introduce CSS pixels, or Density-Independent Pixels (DIP), to the mix. We've used CSS pixels for years without concern, as they map precisely to the physical dots per inch (DPI) on our devices. The second block in Figure 3.2 shows a case where the physical pixels and CSS pixels are 1:1. The third and fourth blocks show cases where the CSS pixels are at 1.5:1 and 2:1 respectively. These align with the current raft of Android and Retina displays.

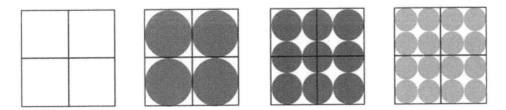

Figure 3.2. Magnified 2x2 pixel blocks with (from right to left) 2x, 1.5x and 1x dots per pixel

We can see from Figure 3.2 that we arrive at the pixel ratio by dividing the physical pixels (the DPI) by CSS pixels (the DIP). Two divided by four gives us a density of 2x on the right, for example. It's worth noting that 2x density will give us four times the number of pixels in the same display area, and the result is an undeniably crisper image. Obviously, with an increase in image quality there is an inherent increase in file weight. Apple claims that its image density is too high for the human eye to make out individual pixels, and this point offsets the increase in bandwidth and file size.

In Figure 3.3, we see the same page displayed in Safari on iOS6 and Chrome on a Retina-capable MacBook Pro. As these are both supported and have **2x** resolution display, they show our **style.png**.

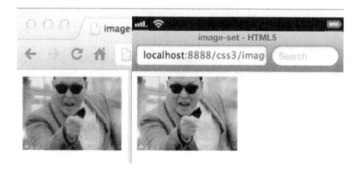

Figure 3.3. image-set on Retina Chrome and iOS6 Safari

We'll see the syntax from `image-set` again in the section called "W3C Adopts `srcset`", but we're yet to see support in enough browsers for us to rely on it, unless of course your target devices are WebKit-only. At least CSS is making inroads towards a solution for adaptive images. Let's now see what JavaScript can do.

Scripted Adaptive Images

So, we've seen that CSS falls short of providing a complete working solution to adaptive images; however, by adding a little JavaScript to the mix, we get much closer. Just like our CSS solutions, JavaScript solutions rely on differing levels of performance, which tend to block the load process of our applications.[1] If we deliver the right image to our device, but at the expense of user experience or page performance, it's clearly not the right solution.

The goal, then, is a solution that can be employed across server variations and intruding as little as possible so that we can focus on our users. A notable example here is Scott Jehl's Picturefill polyfill.[2] A **polyfill** is a code solution that recognizes a gap between a specification and the browser implementation, and seeks to address that gap; it enables us to use emerging technology in otherwise noncompliant browsers. An example is shown in Figure 3.4. In the case of Picturefill, Jehl allows us to experiment with the `picture` element that we'll look at shortly.

---

[1] http://www.stevesouders.com/blog/2009/04/27/loading-scripts-without-blocking/
[2] https://github.com/scottjehl/picturefill

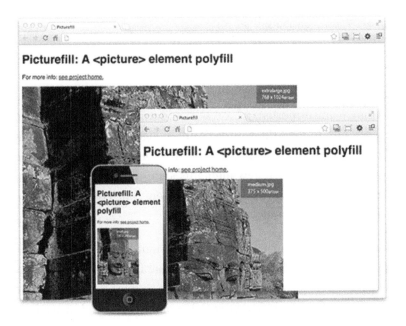

Figure 3.4. Context-aware image sizing using Picturefill

To implement Picturefill, you add a small 0.5KB file to your document head so that it reads through your DOM looking for an element pattern it recognizes. A data-picture attribute on a div triggers the JavaScript and it reads through the data-picture element's child elements, treating them as alternate sources. These sources are then applied using media-query break points to provide images that best fit the user's device, as shown in the code example in Jehl's Git repository:

```
<div data-picture data-alt="A giant stone face at The Bayon temple i
➡n Angkor Thom, Cambodia">
  <div data-src="small.jpg"></div>
  <div data-src="medium.jpg"
    data-media="(min-width: 400px)"></div>
  <div data-src="large.jpg"
    data-media="(min-width: 800px)"></div>
  <div data-src="extralarge.jpg"
    data-media="(min-width: 1000px)"></div>
    <!-- Fallback content for non-JS browsers. Same img src as the i
➡nitial, unqualified source element. -->
  <noscript>
    <img src="small.jpg" alt="A giant stone face at The Bayon temple
```

```
➡ in Angkor Thom, Cambodia">
  </noscript>
</div>
```

The polyfill uses `div` elements over `picture` and source elements (which we'll look into later) as they're unsupported in browsers, and over `img` elements, as the browsers immediately attempt to load the source of any images it finds in the DOM. By avoiding the unsupported elements, Picturefill avoids the performance hit[3] of educating the browser how the new elements should be treated. By failing to download images it won't use, Picturefill better emulates the bandwidth a fully supported native solution would enjoy.

The `data-media` attributes queue the source that should be taken from their `data-src` attribute, and this is applied to an `img` element that is created and inserted into the DOM. It assumes the user has JavaScript enabled in their device. With JavaScript turned off, the image held in the `noscript` element is displayed instead; the fallback is as well-considered as other features of Picturefill.

As a polyfill, Picturefill was never going to be the final solution to the problems adaptive images are setting out to address. It was a way to ease developers into using an experimental code pattern, a way they could show their support. Ideally, a polyfill allows us to deploy code today that the browser will one day be able to utilize without the need for a polyfill at all. While JavaScript enables us to push boundaries when it comes to browser usage, we will be able to reduce our reliance on it when other technologies become available. Like pure CSS-based solutions, JavaScript solutions—even when they're as well-considered as Picturefill—are always going to be superseded by ones that works consistently and natively across browsers. And HTML5 is our go-to for all-browser technology.

HTML5 needed "a markup-based means of delivering alternate image sources based on device capabilities, to prevent wasted bandwidth and optimize display for both screen and print".[4] Let's take a look at how HTML5 is helping us solve adaptive images.

---

[3] http://www.w3.org/community/respimg/2012/03/15/polyfilling-picture-without-the-overhead/

[4] http://www.w3.org/community/respimg/

HTML5 Adaptive Solution

For a large part of 2012, the development community watched with bated breath while two proposals vied for supremacy in how we'd deal with adaptive images in HTML5. One of the popular aims of HTML5 was to try to codify techniques that were found in broad usage. As a result, we now have `nav`, `section`, and `aside` elements in HTML5 due to the large number of those IDs found in the wild. And this approach has served the WHATWG and W3C well, by and large. Where it runs into difficulty, however, is when it attempts to deal with experimental developments in HTML5, or those that lack a broad base of in-the-wild examples to draw from.

As we've seen, adaptive images was one of these developments yet to be solved. It required WHATWG and W3C to establish a new way forward without relying on a hit-and-miss solution using current tools; it needed to be untried.

The Web Standards community was keen to help. It established a solution that could be endorsed and formed the Responsive Images Community Group (RICG), whose web page is shown in Figure 3.5. It then proposed an approach that drew on existing HTML5 markup patterns.

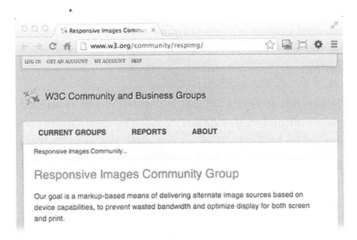

Figure 3.5. The RICG's official group page from the W3C

The strength of its proposal is reinforced by the fact that Bruce Lawson, a Web Standards advocate working at Opera, arrived independently at the same solution, at the same time.[5] Both groups had devised a `picture` element with child source

---

[5] http://html5doctor.com/html5-adaptive-images-end-of-round-one/

elements where each source indicated an image source to be delivered to target devices. The Picturefill solution we've just covered was intending to endorse the `picture` element.

Yet the RICG's approach was overlooked by the WHATWG, and something altogether different was set in the specification. As a result, the community was polarized: advocates for browser manufacturers (such as Apple) faced off against those pushing for what they argue is a better solution.

W3C Adopts `srcset`

Instead of the new `picture` element, a new parameter for the `img` element—the `srcset`—was added to the WHATWG's draft. With the backing of Apple and other browser implementers, the WHATWG's Ian Hickson had opted for a solution that was more likely to make it into our browsers:

```
<img src="logo.jpg" alt="SampleCorp"
  srcset="large.png 600w 200h 1x,
    large_2x-res.png 600w 200h 2x,
    mobile-icon.png 200w 200h">
```

`srcset` was proposed by Apple's Ted O'Connor, based on his `image-set` method that we looked at earlier. A solution for adaptive images was in place, but overlooking the RICG's contribution.

The value of the new attribute is a comma-separated list of image candidate strings, each with a source and up to three descriptors.[6] The descriptors combine to create identifiers for target devices. The first candidate in the example mentioned would target **large.png** to a device that is at least 600px wide and 200px high with a 1x-pixel density.

Public opinion of the `srcset` parameter is mixed. Many claimed it had exposed a side of the HTML5 process that had been better left alone.[7] Others stated that the pattern itself was less robust than the `picture` pattern proposed by the RICG. While many were scathing, some were pragmatic with their analysis.[8] Hickson had imple-

---

[6] http://www.w3.org/html/wg/drafts/srcset/w3c-srcset/#image-candidate-strings
[7] http://adactio.com/journal/5474/
[8] http://cssquirrel.com/comic/?comic=97

mented a solution that had a tested predecessor in `image-set` and which the browser-makers could endorse, rather than the choice more popular with developers.

It would be easy to side with the RICG and point the finger when looking at `srcset`, but that would fail to help us understand the approach better. Let's look at the previous example (with the indented formatting stripped out) where a sample logo image is targeted to two densities and also has a small screen version:

```
<img src="logo.jpg" alt="SampleCorp" srcset="large.png 600w
    200h 1x, large_2x-res.png 600w 200h 2x, mobile-icon.png
    200w 200h">
```

We can simplify it further:

```
<img src="logo.jpg" alt="SampleCorp"
    srcset="large_2x-res.png 2x">
```

That last one looks almost manageable.

Progressive Enhancement Practice

Everyone's browser understands the `img` element, but those same browsers will struggle with the new `srcset` parameter. If that's the case, they'll simply load **logo.jpg** and be none the wiser. Until browsers implement the parameter, we'll simply need to ensure that the default image sourced is practical; using **large_2x-res.png** as the `src` might make sense if your visitors have a Retina display-enabled laptop, but not if they're on an older mobile device. The implementation is coming, but until the browsers are compliant, just think of it as another opportunity to practice progressive enhancement.

Our one-liner basically has three sources associated with it. Two are explicit—the **logo.jpg** and **large_2x-res.png**—and one is implicit: another **logo.jpg**. As soon as you put a value in the `srcset` parameter, you're saying, "If you're unable to meet this requirement, just go ahead and use the `src` value."

You can even use this feature to your visitor's advantage, like so:

```
<img src="logo.gif" alt="SampleCorp" srcset="logo.png">
```

What's being said here is that if your browser is capable of understanding the srcset parameter, we'll serve you the PNG version of our logo. Otherwise, you'll receive the GIF version.

So far, so good. If we omit the density from the srcset, the browser will assume we're talking about 1x, but that should be okay. It becomes trickier, though, when we start working with widths and heights. Include either a width or height in any one of the alternative srcset sources, and straight away you need to ensure that each has that property. It will probably only be a small issue, but we do need to be mindful of it:

```
<!-- invalid as only one srcset has a height parameter -->
<img src="logo.jpg" alt="SampleCorp"
  srcset="large.png 600w 1x,
    large_2x-res.png 600w 200h 2x,
    mobile-icon.png 200w">
```

The RICG had pointed out this requirement as a problem with srcset. HTML5 took great strides to simplify the markup required to code applications, and srcset was running against the grain. Rather than making code easier to read and understand, the proposal was relying on a new syntax and new rules; without browser implementations, this was uncharted waters.[9]

Just how uncharted? On December 28, 2012 the W3C released the Editor's Draft of the srcset extension to HTML.[10] While it's a great resource for browser implementers, it can be tough going otherwise. Still, given that from May (when srcset was announced) to December (when adaptive images were added to the WHATWG Living Standard) we were largely working from a mailing list from Hickson,[11] the way forward is a lot clearer. At least, it's clearer in the sense that we know how browsers should implement the 35-odd steps just to work out which image candidate to use.

Let's see what we can do to cut the 35 steps down to size. Browsers will need to go through all the steps, but we should be able to discern an image source faster. Before we start, we'll split the value of the srcset attribute into comma-separated strings,

---

[9] http://blog.cloudfour.com/the-real-conflict-behind-picture-and-srcset/

[10] http://www.w3.org/html/wg/drafts/srcset/w3c-srcset/

[11] http://lists.w3.org/Archives/Public/public-whatwg-archive/2012May/0247.html

and each of these separated strings becomes a candidate. From there, we perform just four checks to determine which image source to use:

1. First, is there a source with a `width` property—a positive number followed by a lowercase "w"? Always check for `width` first. If there is a `width`, find the widest, and if the browser can display that, discard any sources that have a lower `width`. If the browser is unable to display the widest `width`, find the greatest `width` that can be displayed and discard any other sources with a wider or narrower `width`.

2. Next, do any have a `height` requirement property—a positive number followed by a lowercase "h"? Always check for `height` second. If there is a `height`, find where it is tallest, and if it can be displayed, discard any sources that have a lower `height`. If the tallest `height` can't display, find the tallest `height` that can be displayed, and discard any other sources with a greater or lower `height`.

3. Last, of the remaining sources, find the highest pixel density property—is there a positive number followed by a lowercase "x"? If it's the case, and if it can be displayed, discard any sources that have a lower density. If it can't display the highest density, find the highest density it can display, and discard any sources that have a higher or lower pixel density.

4. If there's no `width` or `height`, skip those checks. And, if there's no pixel density, consider the source has a density of `1x`.

That should leave us with one source, so we'll display that.

It's that simple. We might end up with two or more sources if the sources have the same property requirements, but we're not supposed to code that. If it does happen, the browser should keep the first instance of any matches. It's true that we normally keep the last instance of a duplicated ID, and that the styles cascade so we keep the last declaration or property in CSS, but for `srcset` we keep the first instance.

That's what is in the spec, anyway. We still need to find out what the browsers' implementors do, but the spec is clear, even if it is a bit long. When you distill the spec from 35 to five steps, I'm certain every developer worth their salt will be capable of understanding the syntax, but it might take some getting used to. Apart from `image-set`, which also came from Apple, it's a hybrid syntax that has no precedent, uses a foreign unit pattern, and seems overly prone to errors. But we'll adjust to it.

That said, the possibility for errors with srcset may become the real sticking point. Developers make mistakes. HTML4 inherently allowed for us to make mistakes—it was baked in. HTML5 tried as much as it could to make it harder for developers to make mistakes.

Now, though, srcset has added commas, letters, and a syntax that's inflexible. For srcset, it's all or nothing. And worse, if you malform the syntax, it can produce odd outcomes:

```
<img src="logo.jpg" alt="SampleCorp"
  srcset="large.png 600w 200h 1x,
    large_2x-res.png 600w 200h, 2x,
    mobile-icon.png 200w 200h">
```

The errant comma just before the 2x means that our srcset now has an extra candidate. It's just a single character and an easy typo, but srcset's inflexibility opens us to these types of issues. It means that we now have a new source with no filename, no width, and no height parameters; just the pixel density. Ideally, the browser should discount the candidate. And if the browser matched the 600w and 200h minimums, it should keep the **large.png** as it was the first match, and discount the second candidate, the **large_2x-res.png** file. Remember, though, that we still need to wait to find out what the browsers do, as there's no implementation. However, with the spec published, we should see that change.

The Missed `picture` Element

Let's take a brief look at the adaptive-images element solution we almost had. The RICG held that its picture approach was consistent with existing W3C-endorsed element syntax and quick to understand using the following markup:

```
<picture alt="Responsive Company">
  <source src="logo.png">
  <source src="large.png" media="min-width: 600px">
  <source src="large_1.5x-res.png" media="min-width: 600px,
    min-device-pixel-ratio: 1.5">
  <img src="logo.jpg">
</picture>
```

It works just like the video element from HTML5 and relies on a standard img as a fallback. If your browser is unable to recognize the picture element, it will ignore it and move on to the child elements. It then passes through each child element and attempts to use them. If it fails to recognize the child source elements—such as an older browser would—it would arrive at the fallback content of the `img` element and render that.

The `picture` element would have been backwards-compatible using the existing methods browsers use to parse elements.

If your browser can recognize the `picture` element and those source elements, it would also recognize the `media` parameter. That also comes straight out of the spec for the `video` element[12] (it looks like `picture` was doing its level best to not make waves). You'll recognize the `media` parameter's value as well; they're the media queries that form the third pillar of responsive web design.

And your browser gets even more of a buzz from media queries than you do, as we'll see in Chapter 4. In short, though, a browser checks through the values of the `media` properties and when it encounters a match to its display features, it uses the corresponding `src` of the match as the source of the image.

The RICG thought it was on to something. It had proposed a flexible, comprehensive, and readable solution to the problem of transferring image assets to the broad range of devices that face modern designers. It was done using the building blocks set in place by the W3C, and the RICG was rejoicing. Rejoicing all the way up until the WHATWG completely overlooked its proposal.

Adapting Our Example

Ahead, the road remains rocky for adaptive images. While `srcset` has entered draft status with the W3C, the document itself points out that "(i)mplementors should be aware that this specification is not stable." This warning shouldn't stop us from using the new attribute, being aimed at browser manufacturers, but it means we need to be wary. Our best path forward is to rely on the W3C while adding as little code as possible.

Despite the endorsement from Apple, even Safari is yet to support `srcset`, so we'll need to shim browsers as we did with our JavaScript picture polyfill.

---

[12] http://html5.org/r/724

To give our code the best chance of surviving beyond the polyfill, though, we'll need to ensure that—unlike Picturefill—we use only semantic elements and syntax. With that caveat, removing the polyfill will be much easier and while it's in place, we'll get a better picture of the attribute's future.

Let's look at our Web Directions South example again in Figure 3.6, and apply `srcset` to the speaker avatars. We'll use Boris Smus's `srcset-polyfill`[13] to help us past the problems of browser support as it ticks the boxes for a small footprint and reliance on the semantics from the draft specification.

Figure 3.6. Speaker avatars

Implementing the `srcset-polyfill` is as straightforward as you would hope. You add the new syntax from the draft to your image elements and reference the polyfill JavaScript in your document `head`. The earlier in the document you add the JavaScript, the sooner your images will be affected—you just need to balance the placement with the other files you're including.

---

[13] https://github.com/borismus/srcset-polyfill

chapter03/wds/06_srcset/index.html *(excerpt)*

```
<!DOCTYPE html>
<html lang=en>
  <head>
    <meta charset=utf-8>
    <meta name=viewport content="width=device-width,
      maximum-scale=1.0">
    <script src="libraries/srcset.min.js"></script>
```

With luck, you should have very little to adjust in your HTML. For our WDS example, we're going to remove the inline `width` and `height` parameters. The polyfill actually needs the width for non-WebKit browsers, but this may change over time and adjusting CSS properties in an external sheet is far more accessible. Here's the live code from the site:

```
<section class="speaker">
  <img width="65" height="65" alt="Photo of Craig Sharkie"
    class="photo"
    src="http://static.webdirections.org/webdirections/
      images/speaker_c_sharkie.jpg">
  ⋮
</section>
```

And here's our base for applying the attribute:

chapter03/wds/06_srcset/index.html *(excerpt)*

```
<section class="speaker">
  <img alt="Photo of Craig Sharkie"
    class="photo"
    src="graphics/speaker/c_sharkie.jpg">
  ⋮
</section>
```

All we need to do is add the attribute syntax from the spec—inserting our candidates and descriptors—and we're away:

chapter03/wds/06_srcset/index.html *(excerpt)*

```html
<section class="speaker">
  <img alt="Photo of Craig Sharkie"
    class="photo"
    src="graphics/speaker/c_sharkie.jpg">
    srcset="graphics/speaker/c_sharkie_2hd.png 2x"
    ⋮
</section>
```

As you can see in Figure 3.7, we're only adding a single candidate that will change our image when the user's device can display double-density images. If we wanted to respond to screen size, we'd just go ahead and add descriptors for width or height—or both. And that's it; the polyfill does the rest!

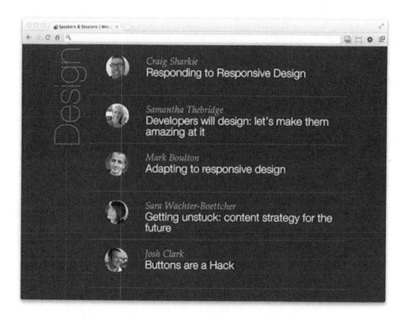

Figure 3.7. Speaker avatars with our new `srcset-polyfill` applied

As we're working with higher density images, we've increased the size of the avatars; the speakers are quite fetching, after all, so that's a nice side effect. It also highlights a consideration with the current version of the `srcset-polyfill`. The JavaScript reads the descriptor and applies a CSS3 scaling property as an inline style:

```
<img alt="Photo of Craig Sharkie" class="photo"
  src="graphics/speaker/c_sharkie_2hd.png"
  srcset="graphics/speaker/c_sharkie_2hd.png 2x"
  style="-webkit-transform: scale(0.5);
    -webkit-transform-origin: 0px 0px;">
```

As this property is applied through a vendor prefix, it has no effect on Firefox:

```
<img srcset="graphics/speaker/c_sharkie_2hd.png 2x"
  src="graphics/speaker/c_sharkie_2hd.png"
  class="photo" alt="Photo of Craig Sharkie">
```

This is fine if the image you want to apply through srcset—such as the one shown in Figure 3.8—is actually twice as large in dimension as it will appear in the UI. If your 2x image is only larger in resolution as it's saved at a higher compression, you'll need to adjust the srcset-polyfill output.

Figure 3.8. One of the fetching WDS avatars for 1x and 2x resolution devices

We also need to transform the image back up to its original size in WebKit, and we do that using a media query that relies on a WebKit-only property. This is best to avoid making a habit of, but while the shim is required to bolster the browsers, it's a must-do.

The end result is as close as we can be to native browser implementation without that implementation actually being there. By using only small amounts of JavaScript and CSS, the page load is impacted as little as possible; when browsers pick up support for srcset, we can remove even that small amount of code gradually.

Get the Picture

We're still not out of the woods when it comes to standardizing a single solution to implement adaptive images across all our browsers, even the most compliant browsers. What we do know is that with the release of the draft specification, browser vendors can start to release implementations of the `srcset` attribute, so we can expect support to grow. In the interim, we can celebrate being part of the standardization process. Our support—or lack of support—for `srcset` can have a material effect on whether the attribute remains in HTML5.

Till then, we have access to a range of CSS, JavaScript, and HTML options that can provide trustworthy solutions to the problem of delivering device-specific image choices. And we can use polyfills to achieve better results as well—whether you're on the `srcset` or picture side of the fence.

Who knows, if the W3C see enough support for the `picture` element, it might mean that the `picture` element makes the picture.

4

Understanding Media Queries

Media queries are the third pillar of responsive web design, and are an extension to HTML5 that allows features of a user's display to determine the CSS delivered to the device, as defined by the CSS3 Module.[1] A mobile device in portrait orientation with a viewport width of 320px can be detected and given different styles compared to a desktop device with a viewport width of 1024px. Conventionally, the different styling would normally be restricted to layout, backgrounds, and images; in essence, a completely new set of styles can be delivered.

As in media types, there are three ways to invoke media-query-dependent styles. First of all, as stylesheets in the `link` element of HTML or XHTML:

```
<link rel="stylesheet" type="text/css" media="all and
   (color)" href="/style.css">
```

Secondly, in XML:

---

[1] http://www.w3.org/TR/css3-mediaqueries/

```
<?xml-stylesheet media="all and (color)" rel="stylesheet"
  href="/style.css" ?>
```

And finally, in CSS stylesheets using @import rules:

```
@import url("/style.css") all and (color);
```

Or using @media rules:

```
@media all and (color) { /* one or more rule sets… */ }
```

Once again, responsive web design is providing the tools to create a fire-and-forget approach that produces layouts we can trust. It leaves us free to concentrate on the content that keeps our users returning to our applications.

As we can see from Figure 4.1, modern devices have vastly distinct capabilities and requirements when it comes to assets and styling. Luckily, the syntax for media queries is straightforward, and is both broadly supported and utilized—in fact, it's made an appearance in each chapter of this book so far!

Figure 4.1. The image assets in their target devices

We typically try to limit the CSS delivered to each target. Starting from styles that are common, we build device-specific styles. But it's not just the styles themselves that we target, there are also the assets delivered by those styles. Figure 4.2 shows that if we send the 1920px-wide background to our 320px-wide display from Figure 4.1, we'll be sending an asset around 14 times larger than required. That's a bandwidth and performance hit to your application that you can easily do without.

Figure 4.2. Our small image fits approximately 14 times in our large image

Let's take a look at a media query that will target the iPhone 5:

```
@media only screen and (min-device-width: 640px) and
  (max-device-width: 1136px) and
  (-webkit-min-device-pixel-ratio: 2) {
    /* iPhone 5 only — at least for now */
}
```

By now, that syntax is going to be looking partly familiar at the least. We've seen device-width in our viewport meta element, and device-pixel-ratio in the picture element from adaptive images. And as if that weren't enough, media queries are the cousins of media types that were released in May 1998 as part of the CSS2.0 recommendation.[2]

Exploring Media Features

You can do a lot with media queries even if you just rely on device-width. Remember, though, that you can look at features other than a device's width. There are currently 13 media features catered for in the specification:[3] width, height, device-width, device-height, orientation, aspect-ratio, device-aspect-ratio, color, color-index, monochrome, resolution, scan, and grid. All but orientation, scan, and grid can accept min- and max- prefixes as well. The level of control you have is refreshing—and a little awe-inspiring!

If you were yet to be in awe of the number of options before you, remember that as the media query features are controlled by CSS, browser vendors can add vendor-prefixed additions to that list; for example, -webkit-device-min-pixel-ratio, which is Apple's addition to enable you to target its Retina devices. And don't forget that there are many more we can access beyond -webkit-:

```
@media only screen and (-webkit-min-device-pixel-ratio: 2)
    and (min-width: 320px),
  only screen and (min--moz-device-pixel-ratio: 2)
    and (min-width: 320px),
  only screen and (-o-min-device-pixel-ratio: 2/1)
    and (min-width: 320px),
  only screen and (min-device-pixel-ratio: 2)
    and (min-width: 320px) {
    /* Small screen retina/amoled styles */
  }
```

Just like standard vendor-prefixed styles, the last property has no vendor prefix in the hope that one day property alone will be enough to reach our target devices.

Gone are the days when handheld would get you out of trouble. Today, you need to consider all your options for targeting devices and judge how to balance your design and development budgets. And that's a judgment that's becoming harder and harder to make with the constant temptation to over-specify queries. With the

---

[2] http://www.w3.org/TR/2008/REC-CSS2-20080411/

[3] http://www.w3.org/TR/css3-mediaqueries/#contents

release of Apple's iPhone 5 with iOS6, the new handset has gained an extra 176px in height. It's unlikely you'd be targeting iPhones using `max-device-height: 960px`—however, if you did, you'd have missed all the iPhone 5s that viewed your application. Consider Figure 4.3.

Figure 4.3. Size comparison of iPhone 4 and iPhone 5 screen heights

True, you can now differentiate iPhone 5 from its predecessors by using `device-height`, but you need to balance that against the possibility that the footer you so painstakingly fixed to the bottom of the screen in iPhone 4S and below will now eerily float 176px above the bottom of the screen. We also need to consider that if the iPhone 5 gained an extra 176px, what can we expect from the iPhone's next generation? Or the one after? Remember our goal: to trust that our style will just work on any device—present or future—without having to rewrite code with each new size.

That being the case, it could be worth a quick look at the syntax we use to pick between features. A media query list is a comma-separated string that uses a series of media queries to target device features:

```
<link rel="stylesheet" media="screen and (color),
    projection and (color)" rel="stylesheet"
    href="example.css">
```

If at least one media query in a media query list is `true`, the list is considered `true` and any `true` feature matches will be honored. For example, if the `screen and (color)` media query in a media query list such as `"screen and (color), projection and (color)"` in the previous code example is `true`, the list is regarded as `true`.

The comma separating each media query expresses a logical OR, and each query can use the `and` keyword to express a logical AND. For the OR query to match, either feature must be present and for the AND query to match, both features must be present. The previous query caters for when your application is viewed on either a screen or projector that's capable of displaying color. If the device falls within that range, it will receive the contained CSS styles.

The `not` keyword can be used to exclude a feature, so this next query will target iPhones but NOT those with Retina displays; it will catch an iPhone 3 but not an iPhone 5, for example:

```
@media only screen (min-device-width: 640px) and
    not (-webkit-min-device-pixel-ratio: 2) {
      /* stylesheet for non-high density phone goes here */
}
```

All in all, the media query syntax is straightforward and can be readily understood and simply read, as long as you keep an eye out for those implicit logical ORs. Had the W3C and WHATWG opted for the `picture` element over the image's `src-set` attribute, the extra exposure that the media query syntax would have gained would have made investment in learning it even more valuable.

Query Feature Support

You can go a long way with media queries concentrating largely on dimension-based features—`width` and `height`, and `device-width` and `device-height`. These have the twin benefits of being both easy to understand and widely supported by browsers. Well, easy to understand as long as you remember that `width` is the width of the browser, and `device-width` is the width the device reports, as shown in Figure 4.4.

Figure 4.4. Comparison of width and device-width

Let's look through the remaining features for an idea of how we can use them:

orientation   accepts either portrait or landscape

aspect-ratio   such as 16:9, or 4:3

resolution   the Dots Per Inch (DPI), or Dots Per Centimetre (DPCM)

scan   a display type that targets televisions that use progressive scanning

grid   matches Teletype displays or devices that only show a single fixed font

monochrome   checks the number of bits per pixel in a monochrome frame buffer, with 0 being falsey

color   checks the number of bits per color of the device, with 0 being falsey

color-index   checks the number of entries in the color lookup table of the device, with 0 being falsey

For a thorough grasp of features, you'll need to master the device's aspect and resolution, which way it is rotated, and whether it displays in color. These are all terms you'd be familiar with when you've created graphics for the Web. Once again, we're back on familiar turf with the HTML5 specification drawing on typical terms[4] when it sets the standard. It makes the learning curve so much more approachable.

While support may vary on features, even the non-dimension-based features are within our reach, as the terminology used is relevant to the target industries. scan and grid might not be immediately obvious to today's desktop-focused designers, but those features are targeted to other devices, and those terms are second nature for developers of such devices. If your work targeted television displays, for example, you'd be well-acquainted with scan and progressive scanning.[5]

What happened to media types?

It's important to remember that while we're concerned here with responsive web design, there are other considerations that can and should impact your application. Just because we're undertaking RWD, doesn't mean we'd overlook accessibility, internationalization, or how your application appears on non-Web displays.

As a result, our queries will most often have screen as the media type, but keep in mind that there are other possibilities![6]

As using media queries and query lists is the best way to understand how to deal with them, let's move on to a practical exercise.

Media Queries in Action

The Web Directions South (WDS) page that has featured throughout our examples already has some media queries straight out of the box. Figure 4.5 shows the masthead graphics that are delivered in turn to browsers that are greater than 800px wide and those less than 800px wide.

---

[4] https://developer.mozilla.org/en/docs/CSS/Media_queries
[5] http://en.wikipedia.org/wiki/Progressive_scan
[6] http://dev.w3.org/csswg/css3-mediaqueries/#background

Figure 4.5. 1565×690px and 800×650px images served via media queries

These graphics ensure that the style of the site is consistent, and, more importantly, that the browsers receiving the assets use as little bandwidth as possible. Our goal? See Figure 4.6.

Figure 4.6. Our goal: the WDS footer at 1440px, 960px, 800px, and 480px widths

The WDS site has media queries applied using a combination of the HTML `link` method and the CSS method. This option ensures that the first point of contact for tracking CSS is in the document `head`, where we're used to seeing linked CSS files. We'll comment them out:

chapter04/wds/index.html *(excerpt)*

```
<!-- <link rel="stylesheet" media="all and (max-width: 800px)"
  href="stylesheets/799max.min.css"> -->
<!-- <link rel="stylesheet" media="all and (min-width: 800px)"
  href="stylesheets/800plus.min.css"> -->
<!-- <link rel="stylesheet" media="all and (min-width: 800px)"
  href="stylesheets/panels.min.css"> -->
```

One caveat to remember using this method is that even linked stylesheets that are unmatched will still download.[7] The unmatched styles won't apply and the assets that are referenced in the unmatched sheets won't download. But the sheets themselves are still downloaded, so can affect your application's performance and bandwidth.

We're actually going to remove all the styling from our example page—a dramatic step, but it will make it easier to restructure our CSS. As the live site focuses its media queries at the top of the page, and simply applies `display: none` when the view becomes narrower than 800px, we're going to focus on the sponsorship section of the page's footer. We'll go back to the removed CSS to find the original styles for the sponsor section and then reset. We just want to restructure the CSS, not reinvent the wheel:

chapter04/wds/index.html *(excerpt)*

```
<link rel="stylesheet" href="stylesheets/reset.css">
<link rel="stylesheet" href="stylesheets/sheet.css">
<link rel="stylesheet" href="stylesheets/query.css">
```

We're going to apply our media queries in our **query.css** file, our default styles in **sheet.css**, and our reset in—you guessed it—**reset.css**. This way, we write as little as possible to our HTML file and rely on sane file naming to help us track our files during maintenance. the section called "Resetting and Normalizing" in Chapter 6 has more information on CSS reset files, so let's concentrate on our default and query files.

As we know, coupling media queries and default style means that we, in effect, gain an extra breakpoint for free in our default style. Let's take a look at the styles we repurposed from the live site to see what we need to alter to set our default. There are 12 styles defined using the `sponsors` ID in their selector, but as luck would have it, we're only going to need to update two of those styles to apply our media queries:

```
#sponsors {
  margin: 2em auto 0 auto;
  width: 800px;
}
```

---

[7] http://scottjehl.github.com/CSS-Download-Tests/

```
#sponsors ul li {
  background-color: #FFF;
  display: inline-block;
  float: left;
  height: auto;
  margin: 0 0 1.7em 0;
  min-height: 120px;
  vertical-align: top;
  width: 30%;
}
```

And of those two selectors, we only need to concern ourselves with declarations around width and margin as altering these creates our responsive breakpoint layouts:

```
#sponsors {
  margin: 2em auto 0 auto;
  width: 800px;
}

#sponsors ul li {
  ⋮
  margin: 0 0 1.7em 0;
  ⋮
  width: 30%;
}
```

First up, let's switch the legacy styles for the styles that will make our footer elements look their best under a mobile-first approach, as demonstrated in Figure 4.7:

chapter04/wds/stylesheets/sheet.css *(excerpt)*

```
#sponsors {
  margin: 2em auto 0 auto;
  width: 480px;
}

#sponsors ul li {
  ⋮
  margin: 0 5px 1.7em 5px;
  ⋮
  width: 470px;
}
```

Figure 4.7. Our footer displayed at 480px

We're on our way. Our first step is to set the `#sponsors` element to always display our mobile-first UI at 480px in width. Because of this, we can hardwire our `li` elements and their margins. We'll switch to a dynamic approach for our breakpoints, but we always know our default style will have a fixed width, and fixed-width elements mean less positioning for the browser to work out. With those changes to **sheet.css**, let's add our first breakpoint in **query.css**:

chapter04/wds/stylesheets/query.css *(excerpt)*

```css
@media only screen and (min-width: 480px) and
  (max-width: 960px) {
    #sponsors {
      max-width: 960px;
      width: 100%;
    }
    #sponsors ul li {
      margin: 0 0.4% 1em 0.8%;
```

```
    width: 31.5%;
  }
}
```

As we're using the @media syntax for targeting our media query, we have our two selectors nested and indented inside the @media rule. Our query list starts with only screen and, then targets displays with min-width: 480px and max-width: 960px, as shown in Figure 4.8.

Figure 4.8. Our footer displayed at 960px

This is our Medium breakpoint. You're right in thinking that we could omit the media type and the min-width feature and still have the same result, but both these features make it easier for us to decipher the breakpoints when we return to maintain our styles. The list could have been shortened to:

```
@media (max-width: 960px) {
    ⋮
}
```

What we gain in brevity, though, we lose in maintainability; the more verbose option actually has a nice payback:

```
#sponsors {
    max-width: 960px;
    width: 100%;
}

#sponsors ul li {
    margin: 0 0.4% 1em 0.8%;
    width: 31.5%;
}
```

The declarations themselves are trusty old CSS. There's no need to change the `margin` on our sponsors element, so there's no declaration for that; instead, we have added a `max-width: 960px`, and we change our `width` value to 100%. As we know from our work on grids, this makes the element fluid, and any screen width between 480px and 960px will have our footer displayed at the largest width possible.

To take advantage of this, we'll also make the `li` elements fluid, giving them percentage-based widths and juggling the percentages to maximize their effect. We want the elements to be as wide as possible without presenting the rounding errors we discussed in the note box, The Devil's in the Detail. If we add the element `width` and the horizontal margins, we end up with: 31.5 + 0.4 + 0.8 = 32.7 percent, giving us a buffer of 0.3 percent to accommodate browser-rounding variations. It's important to remember that outside of you and your team, only a handful of people are going to adjust browser widths to see how your layout responds. Most people are simply going to enjoy the efforts you've gone to in providing them with the best UX possible.

For example, if they were to widen their browser window beyond the 960px threshold as seen in Figure 4.9, they'd invoke the last of our three breakpoints:

chapter04/wds/stylesheets/query.css (excerpt)

```
@media only screen and (min-width: 960px) {
  #sponsors {
    max-width: 1280px;
    width: 100%;
  }
  #sponsors ul li {
    margin: 0 0.5% 1em 0.6%;
    width: 23.5%;
  }
}
```

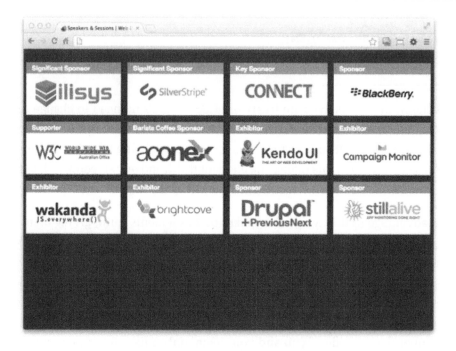

Figure 4.9. Our footer displayed at 1024px

We're using similarly fluid styles for our widest breakpoint, with some nice differences. First up, rather than having the maximum width of our sponsors element the same as the maximum width of our breakpoint, we've given it a hard value of 1280px. This means that any browser width, up to 1280px, will have the element filling the page width. Once it exceeds this width, the sponsors element will only ever be 1280px wide and the margin we applied in our default **sheet.css** style will center the element, as you can see in Figure 4.10.

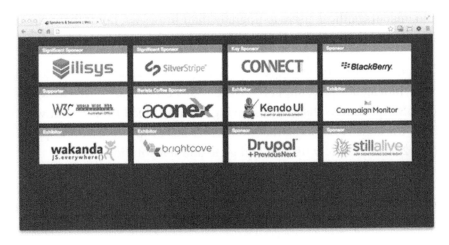

Figure 4.10. Our footer displayed at 1440px

The second change is that we've gone from three sponsors across our UI to four, but we're still using the same fluid approach. Now our total element width is 23.5 + 0.5 + 0.6 = 24.6 percent, giving us a buffer of 0.4 percent. If you were one of those few users who resize their browser window, you'd see the sponsor logos move dynamically from a single column, through three columns, and on to four columns at our widest. The sponsors are happy because we give them the maximum screen real estate at each breakpoint, making their logos more readable, and our users are happy because these readable logos give them the best click target at each breakpoint.

By opting for a combination of breakpoints and fluid layouts, we've optimized our UI for as many factors as possible. We have both sponsors and users on side, and we also have the RWD benefit of not needing to design for every display possible. Where breakpoints can seem like a way for designers to impose control once more on the changing sands of devices, we've opted to work with the breakpoints and not simply jam in a series of fixed layouts.

And as we step off our soapbox, there's only one task left for us to do before the changes are ready for production. The media queries that are making our site appeal to such a broad range of users is actually leaving one user group out in the cold. If your users are still on Internet Explorer earlier than version 9, they'll receive no benefit from your work on media queries at all, as CSS3 was unsupported[8] by IE until version 9. So what are our options?

---

[8] http://caniuse.com/css-mediaqueries

We could encourage those users to upgrade their browsers, but if that were really an option, they'd probably have done it by now.

We could add a JavaScript shim, such as Scott Jehl's Respond.js,[9] which imposes min/max-width media query support on those older browsers. The obvious downside with a JavaScript shim is that we're slowing down the load time of a browser that's already on the slow side. Given that Modernizr has dropped use of Respond.js as of version 2.5, we'll follow its lead and go to another solution.

Our solution revolves around the idea that older versions of Internet Explorer can only be found on desktops. We can use that and IE's conditional comments to provide these browsers with fixed-width layouts, playing to their strengths:

chapter04/wds/index.html *(excerpt)*

```html
<!--[if lt IE 9]>
  <link rel="stylesheet" type="text/css"
    href="stylesheets/ielt9.css">
<![endif]-->
```

And the CSS:

chapter04/wds/stylesheets/ielt9.css *(excerpt)*

```css
#sponsors {
  width: 960px;
}

#sponsors ul {
  padding-left: 3px;
}

#sponsors ul li {
  margin: 0 6px 15px 6px;
  width: 302px;
}
```

The styles we give these browsers are based on our 960px-wide fluid layout, but the layout's converted to fixed width by removing the percentages in favor of known widths and margins. It's what these older browsers (say Internet Explorer, shown

---

[9] https://github.com/scottjehl/Respond

in Figure 4.11) can handle, so we're providing their users with the best possible UX. We're being responsive, and that response is a fixed width.

Figure 4.11. Our footer displayed to older Internet Explorer browsers

Adding Breakpoints

According to the Responsive Images Community Group,[10] a breakpoint is a logical matching of media features that updates the styles of a page: "A single breakpoint represents a rule (or set of rules) that determines the point at which the contents of that media query are applied to a page's layout." It's not the official specification, but it's almost as hard to decipher.

If you think about breakpoints as the points at which your design will break, you are bound to gain a faster grip on what you're dealing with. Let's look at the WDS example again. As we can see in Figure 4.12, when the browser shrinks to 960px wide, and a four-column layout would break, our breakpoint is triggered and we shift to our three-column layout.

[10] http://usecases.responsiveimages.org/#design-breakpoints

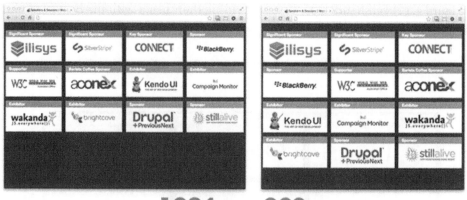

1024px 960px

Figure 4.12. At 960px wide, our WDS four-column layout snaps to our three-column variant

Sure, this is a single rule, but breakpoints don't become harder when you add them together, they just multiply. And of course, our device-targeted sheets will go beyond just the one. Far from it! Even just using device widths for comparison, you might be tempted to consider as many as six breakpoints: 320px, 480px, 600px, 768px, 1024px, and 1280px.

Using just these breakpoints, you'd be able to target a broad range of devices with the current standard widths, in pixels:

320px	mobile portrait
480px	mobile landscape
600px	small tablet
768px	tablet portrait
1024px	tablet landscape/netbook/desktop
1280px and greater	desktop large

With those sizes in mind, your `link` elements might look more like this:

```
<link rel="stylesheet" media="only screen
  and (max-device-width: 320px)" href="tiny.css">

<link rel="stylesheet" media="only screen
  and (max-device-width: 480px)" href="small.css">

<link rel="stylesheet" media="only screen
  and (max-device-width: 960px)" href="medium.css">
```

```
<link rel="stylesheet" media="only screen
  and (max-device-width: 1024px)" href="large.css">

<link rel="stylesheet" media="only screen
  and (min-device-width: 1280px)" href="extralarge.css">
```

Choosing your CSS breakpoints can be tricky: too many and maintenance becomes too difficult, but too few leads to poor UI rendering on devices you don't cater for. At a minimum, you should be looking at two breakpoints: Small, for anything under 480px wide, and everything Bigger. This is mobile first.

Once you have those two working, the question is what to do with the Bigger displays? Let's look at how we break up the bigger ones into Medium, Large, and Extra Large.

Medium would be everything from 480px up to about 960px—that's the 960px we know from our work with grids. Increasingly, this covers people with larger displays that don't use full-screen browser windows, as well as those using a wide range of tablet devices including iPads and Kindles. The `viewport` `meta` element from Chapter 1 really comes into its own here, adapting our 960px layout to work seamlessly on smaller displays such as the iPad's 768px-wide portrait view:

```
<meta name="viewport" content="width=device-width,
  initial-scale=1.0">
```

Our Large breakpoint covers most desktops, laptops, and tablets in landscape mode. It starts from 960px and goes through to 1280px. This leaves us with Extra Large, which is anything greater than 1280px, and accounts for the now standard 20-inch-plus desktop monitor, widescreen higher-end laptops, and emerging tablets.

Three of those breakpoints administered through media queries, coupled with another free breakpoint as a default style for either mobile or desktop, gives us four screen groups, shown in Figure 4.13. These will provide a good range of support for the majority of our users.

Figure 4.13. Our four breakpoints and the devices they target

Beyond that, we quickly reach a point of diminishing returns, and it becomes a matter of balancing the return on investment we can gain from adding more and more breakpoints. We could add a Tiny breakpoint for screens under 320px wide, or even add an "intermediate" breakpoint at 768px, and split our Medium to target lower-end 7-inch tablets. As phones and tablets are moving to higher density displays and capabilities, creating breakpoints with this level of granularity will likely increase your maintenance workload for little payoff. However, if you're building applications for a very diverse set of mobile users (with potentially older or lower spec devices); supporting tiny and intermediate displays may be justifiable.

Balancing Breakpoints

You need to consider which devices you're targeting and balance the possible return gained against how your users are accessing your applications. That balance is important enough if you're only considering a few breakpoints, or even a mixture of the five breakpoints listed above: Tiny, Small, Medium, Large, and Extra Large.

Addressing that balance becomes even more important when you leave the safety of broad breakpoints and start to tackle a more device-specific set.

For many use cases, even most, three of our five named breakpoints will give you the coverage you need. Still, your application may benefit from a more granular approach. Let's look at a solid set of media queries that will target a very broad range of devices, even without concerning ourselves too deeply with Retina or AMOLED devices. Developing styles and designs against these 12 breakpoints would be a Herculean task, and maintaining this many breakpoints would be no less daunting:

```
/* SMALL ANDROID, FEATURE PHONE - PORTRAIT */
@media only screen and (max-width: 240px) {
  ⋮
}

/* SMARTPHONES - PORTRAIT & LANDSCAPE */
@media only screen and (min-device-width: 320px)
  and (max-device-width: 480px),
  only screen and (min-width: 320px) and (max-width:
  480px) {
  ⋮
}

/* SMARTPHONES - LANDSCAPE */
@media only screen and (min-width: 321px) {
  ⋮
}

/* SMARTPHONES - PORTRAIT */
@media only screen and (max-width: 320px) {
  ⋮
}

/* IPADS, TABLETS - PORTRAIT & LANDSCAPE */
@media only screen and (min-device-width: 768px)
  and (max-device-width: 1024px),
  only screen and (min-width: 768px) and (max-width:
  1024px) {
  ⋮
}

/* IPADS, TABLETS - LANDSCAPE */
@media only screen and (min-device-width: 768px)
```

```
    and (max-device-width: 1024px)
    and (orientation: landscape) {
      ⋮
}

/* IPADS, TABLETS - PORTRAIT */
@media only screen and (min-device-width: 768px)
  and (max-device-width: 1024px) and (orientation:
  portrait) {
    ⋮
}

/* TABLETS, DESKTOPS & LAPTOPS */
@media only screen and (min-width: 960px) {
    ⋮
}

/* DESKTOPS & LAPTOPS */
@media only screen and (min-width: 1024px) {
    ⋮
}

/* DESKTOPS & LAPTOPS */
@media only screen and (min-width: 1224px) {
    ⋮
}

/* LARGE SCREENS */
@media only screen and (min-width: 1824px) {
    ⋮
}

/* RETINA & AMOLED DISPLAY */
@ media only screen and (-webkit-min-device-pixel-ratio:
  1.5), only screen and (min-device-pixel-ratio: 1.5) {
    ⋮
}
```

This will certainly keep your team busy and present a challenge. It would be much better to keep the team busy with a smaller number of breakpoints and have them actively look to deprecate any older ones, as support costs outweigh usefulness. Should you find that the named breakpoints we've adopted fall short of properly suiting your needs, you can readily draw your own set from the pool of 12.

Arguably, if you're focusing on the mobile market, you could expect a range of breakpoints to maintain, but rationalizing the number of breakpoints you take on is just as important as taking on board the media query syntax. The only hard-and-fast rule about how many breakpoints to adopt is that you should stop adding breakpoints when you're happy with the number of satisfied users you have.

Rise to the Occasion

Of the technical pillars of responsive web design, media queries are the best established and supported. Additionally, they offer a solid return on investment from a design perspective, and can be applied to existing applications to great effect.

While it's true that legacy support on noncompliant browsers is light, the fact that those browsers are impossible to find outside the increasingly narrow environment of the desktop limits the impact.

Being CSS-based, where we find media queries in compliant devices, the opportunity for experimentation by browser manufacturers has led to a level of control that highlights the power of vendor-prefixed selectors. Of course, this level of control means that the temptation to apply more and more breakpoints through media queries can be hard to resist. That said, resisting the urge to overcommit to breakpoints and simply apply fixed layouts within your breakpoints provides designers with the potential to create superb user-focused solutions.

Your future self will thank you if you avoid overcommitting to too many breakpoints and focus on just the right number. You'll keep your media queries more manageable, and be able to focus on a great UX for the breakpoints you have.

Responsive Content

Content is a fairly broad and murky concept, so here's a definition for our purposes.

*"**Content**" is everything that a user of the site consumes when they interact with your service.*

Using this definition, content means everything from imagery through to navigation, features, forms, words, and video. Limiting our view to just the data that sits inside the `main-col` div is insufficient. Taking a consumption-based view allows us to consider non-human users of our content such as bots and other programs as well.

Responsive Content (RC), then, is a way of making the content on our site adapt or morph based on the behavioral context of the user.

The most obvious example of this in practice is displaying different layouts, information, or features for users of mobile devices compared to users of desktop machines. There's no need to be limited to just the device context, however; our content could respond based on whether a person is brand new to the service or an expert user. For instance, consider how Twitter leads new users through adding accounts to their feed when they sign up to get novice users active quickly, as shown in Figure 5.1.

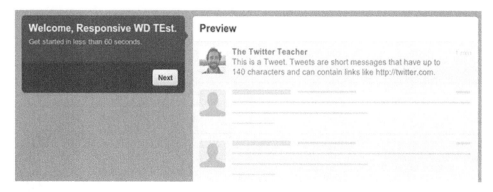

Figure 5.1. The start of Twitter's New User walk-through process

Conversely, GitHub provides command-line functionality for common functions for expert users in their search box, as shown in Figure 5.2.

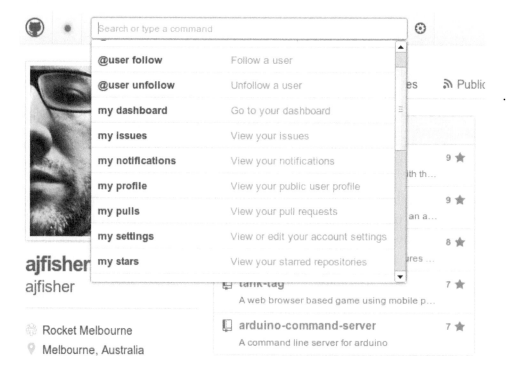

Figure 5.2. GitHub's search box doubles as a "command line"

There is some contention about whether responsive content is a "real thing" or not.[1] Influential designer Mark Boulton comes down on the "not" side very eloquently;

---

[1] http://www.markboulton.co.uk/journal/responsive-content-is-not-a-thing

however, this may be because as a designer who's worked a lot with print and type, he intrinsically thinks about content first. If using the angle that responsive content makes the project team discuss, consider, and strategize better in order to design more appropriate, tailored experiences, that's definitely positive (and this is probably in line with Boulton's view on crafting a responsive system).

Focusing on content first will improve your site. Ensuring that your content is right lifts the experience as dramatically as good design and well-implemented technology.

So, how does content fit into the new responsive world? Do we simply write code that rips out any Flash videos in our CMS so that our content "works" for those pesky mobile browsers? Maybe we just arbitrarily choose a character limit for our content and truncate it? (Hint: This is rarely a good idea, even as a last resort.)

Different requirements drive different solutions. In some cases, thinning down your copy will be appropriate; in others, it won't. The point is that you need to actively explore the options and make a decision—that's what the design process is all about, and content is no exception.

Structured Content Sets You Free

Structure is the key to making your content responsive. Having nicely structured content gives you the ability to reuse and reorganize the way your content behaves in many new ways and on different platforms.

Writing is a structured process. Every time you write you deal with structure: words, punctuation, sentences, paragraphs—all the way through to your content having an appropriate beginning, middle, and end.

Using sensible structure can help aid the origination process as it provides a framework. Without a structure, our content ends up unusable. If we impose arbitrary or ill-considered structure, it then becomes just rules that must be followed—and no one likes rules.

So when we're talking about structure, we'll consider these areas:

- document structure
- metadata
- supporting content

Helping your authors understand these concepts while utilizing a robust structure will make your content much more capable of being responsive (now and into the future) and sets it free.

Document Structure

Let's start with the content we're authoring directly and consider the structure that sits within it. Authoring is never just putting words or links on a page randomly. There's always a need to organize our thoughts in order to communicate them. The funny thing is, the Web actually does this really well these days; we have semantic tags to work with so we can break content up into articles, sections, and paragraphs, as well as having headers and footers. Educating your authoring team on the native capabilities now available in HTML5 will give them the ability to structure their content in greater detail than they can in most word processors.

Logical Blocks

Working in logical blocks makes the content more "chunkable"—that is, allowing it to be broken up in various ways for different use cases. Using the right semantic elements helps here, as it allows us to ascribe meaning to the block we're looking at; a paragraph is distinct from a heading, for example.[2]

For the WDS speakers page we can look at a speaker as being a logical component, but it also contains a group of logical subcomponents, as demonstrated in Figure 5.3: a photo (1), a name (2), the session title (3), a biography (4), a Twitter handle (5), and a session description (6).

---

[2] This excellent video from Karen McGrane talks about adapting your process to "adaptive" content. http://aneventapart.com/news/post/aea-video-karen-mcgrane-adapting-ourselves-to-adaptive-content

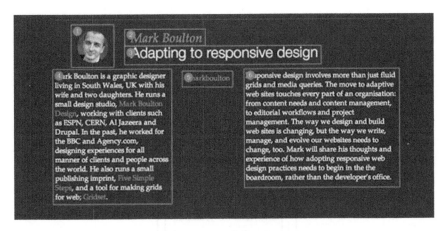

Figure 5.3. One speaker has six logical subcomponents

By providing good structure around these components, they can be rearranged from a layout standpoint however we like for different contexts.

This logical modularity is a key feature of design and development for the Web. Doing the same thing with content plays to the Web's strengths and allows for reuse or a recombination of our content in different ways without having to rewrite everything from scratch each time.

A good example is being able to split content across multiple pages. The news industry has done this for a variety of reasons concerning advertising, but being able to arbitrarily paginate a really long article has benefits for mobile users where page rendering will be slower. The converse of this is that the same process allows for "infinite scrolling," such as that seen on Twitter or Tumblr feeds. Being able to provide these types of experiences is all down to having highly modular "chunks" of content.

Hierarchy

Bots, CSS, and developers all love content that's ordered by hierarchy. Hierarchy makes it really easy to assign precedence when you need it. The ability to say this heading is a Level 1 and this one is a Level 2 is handy, but also being able to say that this paragraph belongs to this section, which belongs to this article, is a powerful way of being able to structure content and make it more portable.

Let's look at the example from our WDS speakers page, stripped down to its bare structure in Figure 5.4. Here, a speaker is a self-contained unit that can be moved around on the page or syndicated to other pages or systems. It contains other units of information such as images, biographies, and session details, but these all belong to a particular speaker.

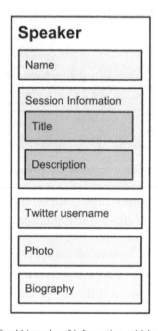

Figure 5.4. A speaker has a defined hierarchy of information, which can in turn have subhierarchies

A speaker then belongs to a "track," such as Design or Development. This imposed hierarchical system allows for the tracks to be moved around as individual units as well.

Hierarchy enables us to organize content, beyond it simply being a random assortment of logical objects in a document.

Metadata

Metadata is more than just those elements you threw into your head section to help search engines understand what's on the page. Rather, it's descriptive information about the content, and it can exist at varying levels in the content hierarchy. A speaker can be part of a track that's on the sessions page, and all three of those content pieces can have their own metadata.

Let's consider each of those content pieces and think about the metadata that could be applied to them. We'll represent the content items and metadata as JSON (we could also use XML just as easily) in order to think about it without being distracted by the HTML structure and formatting.[3]

At the page level, we have some fairly traditional metadata: who authored the page, when was it created, when was it last updated, what is its review date, and whether the page has a target rendering type. It appears as follows:

```
{
  "page": {
    "tracks": [
      "Design",
      "Development",
      "Big Picture",
    ]
  },
  "name": "Web Directions South 2012",
  "tags": "Event, Conference",
  "Author": "Maxine Sherrin",
  "lastupdated": "201209160300Z10",
  "created": "201204160300Z10",
  "nextreview": "201211160300Z10",
  "publicationtargets": [
    "Desktop",
    "Mobile",
    "Tablet",
  ]
}
```

What about the metadata for a track? If all the sessions were occurring in one location, we could include the location here. We could also include tags that describe the overall theme of the track or descriptors that help to classify it (for example, "Design" in this case means web design, so that could be included as a classifier).

Here's a sample of how we might describe the track:

```
{
  "track": {
    "sessions": [
      "session_id1",
      "session_id2"
```

---

[3] See Wikipedia for a good starting point: http://en.wikipedia.org/wiki/JSON

```
    ]
  },
  "name": "Design",
  "tags": "Design, Web Design, Information Architecture, Responsive
➥Design, Content",
  "Location": "Sydney Convention Centre, Sydney, Australia"
}
```

And here's a sample of what a session and a speaker entry might look like (bio and session details truncated for brevity):

```
{
  "session": {
    "title": "Getting unstuck: content strategy for the future",
    "sessiontime": "201210160300Z10",
    "location": "Sydney Conference Centre, Main Stage.",
    "description": "Responsive. Adaptive. Mobile first. Cross-channe
➥l. We all want a web that's more flexible, future-friendly, and re
➥ady for unknowns...",
    "slidenotes": " http://www.slideshare.net/Saraboettcher/getting-
➥unstuck-content-strategy-for-the-future",
    "postvideo": " http://www.youtube.com/watch?v=bPAamdlwQ94",
    "livestream": "",
    "track": "Design",
    "tags": "RWD, Responsive Design, Content, IA, UX, Design",
    "speaker": {
      "name": "Sara Wachter-Boettcher",
      "twitter": "sara_ann_marie",
      "bio": "Sara Wachter-Boettcher is an independent content strat
➥egist, writer, and rabble-rouser based in Lancaster, Pennsylvania.
➥She got this way after stints as a journalist, copywriter, and web
➥ writer, during which she became increasingly dissatisfied with th
➥e chaos typically found in web content projects... .",
      "blog": "http://sarawb.com",
      "photo": "speaker-s-wachter-boettcher.jpg"
    }
  }
}
```

The basic session and speaker details have been enhanced with the following metadata:

▪ session times in a machine-readable format (including time-zone information)

- descriptive data added using tags to classify the session

- location information allowing physical locations to be shown

- information about media streams and slide notes to provide reference materials after the session has completed

With some further thought, other metadata could be added without too much trouble. The key is to be consistent. Making metadata easy to manage is one part of the process; the other is creating a work flow that supports its creation and limiting the sort of content that can be published without it.

Now that we have our content structured with some metadata, we can start looking at different ways to display it to the user based on context, such as in Figure 5.5.

Figure 5.5. Mobile (and desktop) users can have optimized experiences of content

The same content can be used during the conference to create a What's On guide, as shown in Figure 5.6.

Figure 5.6. Content that helps attendees locate the sessions they're interested in

These are just a couple of examples, but all use the same core metadata in different ways.

Supporting Content

Supporting content is neither metadata nor core content. Some examples of supporting content are:

- most media assets
- mantles or subheads
- call-outs or pull quotes
- citations and references

This is the sort of content that enriches an experience (particularly on the Web, where we can have multiple layers of content so easily), but does no harm to the core content when absent. Explicitly denoting these types of content as "supporting content" helps with creating a more modular, logical structure.

In many documents, this type of content is buried inside the core content itself when it shouldn't be. It's often this type of content that causes the most problems when you try to update a site's design, because it has formatting or other code to support it. Make sure that all supporting content stored is linked to but separate from your core content, and you will find it easier to reuse it in different ways—this is the knack of making your content "chunkable."

Technical Approaches to Responsive Content

You've decided that parts of your content needs to be responsive, and your authors are doing a fantastic job creating content that is highly structured with rich metadata; now that content needs to be rendered somewhere on the Web. The following techniques should help for a range of different scenarios to assist you in adapting your content.

 Real-world Application

Many of the techniques needed for responsive content require a server-side approach to make them work, including modifications to the CMS being used. Rather than dwell on a particular platform or framework, or look in detail at one CMS, we'll focus on the core concepts of what we're trying to achieve. All of these techniques are relatively commonplace across most platforms, so there should be existing examples for you to use for implementation.

Remove Contextually Bad Content

Sometimes you need to remove content as a first step rather than as the last resort it really should be. The key here is to craft a better experience by removing obstacles or annoyances for your users.

Here is where removing content is appropriate:

- anytime the user is unable to display the content (for example, Flash files for an iOS device)

- heavy assets where the user is in a resource-constrained context (for example, HD video to a mobile user on a 3G network)

- whenever the content fails to gracefully re-render or just breaks (for example, some ads not designed for mobile devices render full size and may not work at all)

- where no assumed device context exists (for example, using the DeviceMotion Event API on a desktop computer that is without an accelerometer)

In the case where a page component is structural (for example, site navigation) or core to the interaction a user should be taking (for example, a button that you want the user to click), you should never just remove it. Under these conditions, you'll need to create an alternative in order to maintain the experience.

For the best user experience, if you need to remove content for the reasons cited here, you should remove it entirely from the document before the browser even sees it. The browser will still download content that's hidden using CSS.

Using data- attributes in your markup allows you to provide hints to the server about when content should be removed for a particular target. For example:

```
<img src="really-really-really-big-file.jpg" data-target="full"
  data-action="remove">
```

In this case, the image is clearly enormous and intended for the "full" desktop experience. All other targets should have this element removed.

If you are publishing static content for different targets (using Jekyll,[4] for example), this works well. Using this content removal technique on the fly, however, will cause serious performance degradation.

 HTML5 Video Is King

We're at the point where HTML5 video can be used in preference over Flash in most circumstances. Deliver HTML5 video as the standard in all your video embeds and then degrade back to Flash as needed.[5] However, you should also look at

---

[4] http://jekyllrb.com/
[5] http://www.sitepoint.com/html5-video-cross-browser-fall-backs/

what your authors are embedding in the CMS as sometimes the older embeds of YouTube or Vimeo clips (does anyone actually self-host video anymore?) will default to Flash.

Dynamic Loading by Context

Let's assume that all users will utilize the same site regardless of their device. We're going to use purely responsive techniques to render our content. We've already created some well-structured HTML for it to live in and we're using the pillars of media queries, adaptive images, and grids to lay out our content appropriately. Can we do anything else to help make the content more responsive?

Lazy Loading

The **Lazy Load** technique allows you to improve the loading speed of a page by only loading images that are visible to the viewport.[6] As the user scrolls down, other images can be loaded as needed. All the assets will eventually be used, but this is a more intelligent way to serve them—particularly to bandwidth-constrained users.

Selective Content Loading

Selective Content Loading (SCL) is where you load small amounts of content into the page after a user requests a link, rather than the whole shebang each time. This can result in significant performance improvements, particularly in bandwidth-constrained contexts such as a mobile phone on a poor network.

Conceptually, this is how it works:

1. On the first page request, we load all the page content including the site navigation, content, CSS, and JavaScript files.

2. After the page has loaded, instead of standard requests, we override all the links in our page to make XMLHttpRequests (XHRs).

---

[6] This is a good, mobile-friendly example of using lazy loading: http://www.metaltoad.com/blog/improved-lazy-loading-mobile-devices-iphone-android-lazy-load-17.

3. We then process the response (the XHR response will only be the internal page content rather than the entire page) and overwrite the content that was in the page in conjunction with a template.[7]

4. We can then use `pushState()` from the History API to modify our browser history (so that the URL updates to a relevant link that can be shared and we can navigate backwards through our browser history if need be).

Keep in mind that SCL won't work in every circumstance and can cause issues. Without care, your URL structure can break, or you may end up with pages without any content on them that are then examined by search spiders.

Remember, the entire HTML needs to be loaded, whether you use it or not. With SCL, you're trying to optimize the speed from a click to the next page of content for the user; providing templates for every possible page type when the user loads the first page may outweigh the gains you make in selective content loading later.

Selectively loading content for pages similar to the one the user is currently on provides a good balance in most cases (for example, a speakers page could use SCL to load other speakers, but not load FAQs).

When you have very similar content in a stream (for example, status updates in a feed or multiple pages of a long news article), you can use SCL to create an infinite-scrolling experience. Here, SCL is used to continually add more content to the end of the stream as the user reaches it, as there's no need to make a full-server round-trip for the "next page."

 Server Implications

Going down a mixed-request route opens up some possible server-side issues you need to be aware of. Traditionally, web application servers take a request and fetch the data needed to fulfill it, then combine it with a structured template to create HTML that's sent to the client for rendering. Unless all your content is accessible via an API, you're going to have to add code to determine whether the request is a "real" page request or an XHR. Many modern web frameworks such

---

[7] Handlebars.js is very good for this type of templating: http://handlebarsjs.com.

as Django help with this,[8] but older applications servers don't, which may limit your options.

Platform-specific Experiences

If you have well-structured content that is available through an API as well as the capability in your organization, you can create platform-specific experiences for your users. Typically, this would start with mobile and desktop users, but tablet experiences are becoming increasingly common as well.

For a platform-specific experience, you will deliver entirely different HTML, CSS, and JavaScript to the users based on their context. The same base content will be used, but it will be rendered differently for each context.

The biggest benefit here is that you can now craft your core templates with platform-specific optimizations. The standard way to do this is to define a set of core contexts and then apply RWD principles to each core context individually. So we could define our contexts as "Desktop," "Mobile," and "Tablet."

Within each of these core contexts, we can then use the RWD pillars to adjust for the variation within that particular context (for example, landscape- and portrait-mode cell phone displays, or the variety of tablet sizes we're now seeing). As we're creating unique templates, we can go further and use optimized libraries for each context if appropriate; so we could use jQuery on desktop, but Zepto[9] for mobile. This allows us to choose and apply the best techniques for a particular context to deliver a great experience.

Domain Decisions

We should try to avoid changing our URIs.[10] There are good reasons for this, such as search engines not knowing which URI is canonical if content is duplicated and ensuring your users know where to go. Many web applications (Google included) use multiple domains in order to provide different platform experiences more easily.

---

[8] Django (www.djangoproject.com) with TastyPie (https://github.com/toastdriven/django-tastypie), which is used to create APIs around your views, is an extremely powerful combination and creates a huge opportunity for your content to be reused.

[9] http://zeptojs.com/

[10] Tim Berners-Lee on the matter: http://www.w3.org/Provider/Style/URI.html

If you need to serve content from multiple domains (for example, www.example.com and m.example.com) and your content is essentially the same on each domain, you should maintain the rest of your URI pattern so that they match; so m.example.com/path/to/file and www.example.com/path/to/file should mean the same, content-wise. The former would give the content to you rendered for mobile, the latter for desktop.

The benefit of multiple domains is that you can use different application servers to deliver the site and keep them independent, allowing you to make architectural decisions around how each context is working (for example, caching, app server needs, and so on).

There's a subtle user benefit here as well in that you can tell users to go to m.example.com as the mobile destination in your marketing material, signaling that you have a specific mobile experience for them. The effects of this will wear off soon, though, because users are coming to expect it.

Sometimes you'll deliver totally unique experiences, so matching the paths in a URI from one domain to the other will make no sense; for example, m.example.com/mobile/only/page versus www.example.com/desktop/only/page. If this describes your scenario, you should ensure any content that's the same across contexts has matching URI patterns; where content differs, an alternative URI structure is used. This should help alleviate confusion with users, bots, or other consumers of your content.

Browser Routing

If you reach the point of having two (or more) domains serving content, you'll quickly run into the issue of having to select one for a user who has hit the site from the "wrong" type of device.

Depending on what web servers you are using and the exact nature of your setup, there are many ways to do this. From an algorithmic standpoint, Figure 5.7 describes how you would approach routing the browser.

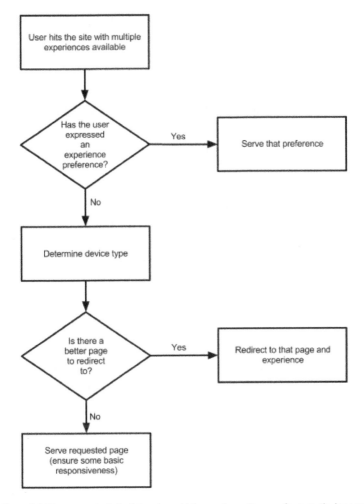

Figure 5.7. The process to help determine which experience to serve for a particular page

Here it is explained in more detail:

1. If the user has expressed a session-based or overall preference for a particular experience, acknowledge that preference and serve the experience they have asked for. Always provide a clear option to change this preference.

2. Detect what type of device the user has (user-agent checking is one way, but you can use media queries and JavaScript to confirm and then force a redirect). If in doubt, assume they are mobile users, as there's significantly more variation than on desktops. It also impacts the UX more to send a mobile user to the desktop site than a desktop user to the mobile site.

3. If the user is on the "wrong" site for the device, check if there is an equivalent page on the "correct" site for them (this is easy if you use a direct URI mapping, as all pages should exist). If there is, redirect them to the correct page with an HTTP redirect.

4. If there is no equivalent page to redirect them to, provide the user with the page they requested. Avoid redirecting them to the destination domain 404 page or home page. The user hasn't made an error, but your application will by redirecting them to a page that doesn't exist.

5. Ensure that your desktop site has at least some basic media queries in place; that way, if a mobile user arrives at a desktop page, this last-resort option will suffice.

6. Provide an option on every page (in the footer, for example) to switch to an alternate version. If the user clicks this, make sure that they're switched to the right version for at least the duration of their session (unless they otherwise force a change).

If you follow these rules, a user should be served the best possible experience—even in failure. Pay particular attention to point 4 about redirecting them to a failure page. Most mobile users have experienced redirection failure at some point; it's particularly common on sites whose mobile and desktop URIs aren't completely synchronized.

Template Routing

Template routing is where you use a single domain to serve your content and provide a full template (HTML, CSS, JavaScript, and so on) that's particular to the context.

All users access the same domain and application logic; however, they are served templates that are completely specific to their platform, as shown in Figure 5.8.

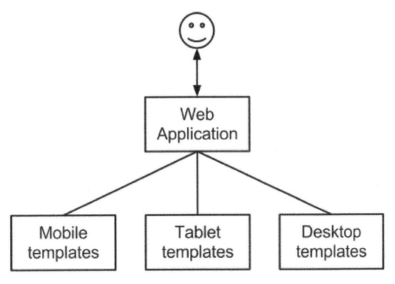

Figure 5.8. Serving content specific to mobile, tablet, and desktop

Template routing only works in scenarios where you have your entire site and all its functionality represented in each context (that is, rather than serving completely different types of experience, you're serving the way those experiences are rendered).

To do this, you need to have your templates and content fully separated. Modern development frameworks like Django[11] and Ruby on Rails[12] enforce this strongly using MVC (Model, View, Controller), so this is quite easy to achieve. PHP[13] and .NET[14] have similar options available to them.

In this scenario, the View provides all the application's business logic and user interaction, leaving the static content to the Controller to determine how it's rendered. In a standard application, this means establishing what type of device is accessing the site (say mobile, tablet, or desktop), and then choosing the appropriate template to employ in rendering the content.

The benefits of template routing are:

■ A single domain is used for all users (including bots).

---

[11] http://www.djangoproject.com

[12] http://rubyonrails.org/

[13] http://www.tinymvc.com/

[14] http://www.asp.net/mvc

- Each platform can still have a specific experience.

- There is no wastage of content delivered and left unused (due to it being inappropriate for the platform).

- Different user experience aspects can be prioritized according to context.

- All application logic is maintained in one place.

Once you start going down this path, other options become available as a result, such as thinking about different types of contexts and the templates that support them. For example, while still having the same fundamental View logic, you could create a Controller set of templates specifically for "New Users" that's tuned to their specific needs.

The Cotton On mobile site, shown in Figure 5.9, prioritizes search to move users to products quickly, whereas the desktop and tablet sites show greater product range and promotions due to the larger format. Both are driven by the same content and the same domain with different templates for the different contexts.

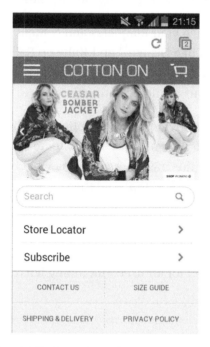

Figure 5.9. The Cotton On mobile site prioritizes search

Determining How Far to Go

Rather than deciding to make every part of your content responsive, a wise starting point is to set some boundaries; for example, tackling one additional platform to start. Gaining experience and learning from success and failure will help shape the way you enhance the responsiveness of your systems over time. The only way to do this is to bring the business you work for on the journey.

This checklist should help you decide how far you can go and what you could achieve.

What benefits or solutions does responsive content solve for the users?

The user always comes first. Prioritize content and functionality according to how your users want to experience your service.

What content skills are available in the team?

Responsive content often means adding at least more structure to your content, even if producing new content is unnecessary. Do you have the staff or the skills to do this? Will you need to train authors or put new processes in place to support them?

You should also determine whether writers having HTML skills is a worthwhile goal. (Hint: web skills are in high demand everywhere, so pitch it as career building if you hit resistance.)

What can be achieved with the technical platform?

Many CMSs have been designed without consideration for responsive content at all, especially large-scale "enterprise" solutions that are heavily geared towards desktop content. Most CMSs are aimed at making the authoring process as "deskilled" as possible, so that there's no requirement for people with HTML skills to edit pages. Assessing your technical platform's capabilities will determine whether changes need to be made to it or not.

Should you have tuned content, or different experiences entirely?

This is a hard decision and one that will cause a lot of debate. The big question here is how much of your service is relevant in *every* context for your users. Understanding what your users are likely to use in different contexts helps drive the decisions around content tuning.

If you do tune your experience by limiting functionality or content in one context, ensure that you give the user the option to reach the "full" version.

How are your users interacting already? Be guided by the existing data in order to give you context.

Where you can, use data to help you make decisions about how to change the content based on user context. Looking at common user journeys already being undertaken when your site is yet to be optimized for different platforms will provide good insight into what people want to do in that context.

Tailor Made

Making your content responsive is as much about training your authors and modifying your content production processes as it is about technical or design implementation. It will be hard the first time you do this, but the end rewards will be worth it: you'll likely be saved from having to do it again, and you'll be making your content usable in new contexts while being future-friendly.[15]

The key points to remember are:

- Start from the user and work backwards to the content and systems. How does the user want to experience the content and in what context are they experiencing it (mobile versus desktop, high-speed connection versus narrowband mobile, new versus expert user, and so on)?

- Are you able (technically and process-wise) to deliver different site experiences on different domains to your users? If not, ensure your HTML is as minimal as possible and load in extra content for high-end users.

- Always make sure that your URIs consistently map across all your services. Never redirect a user to a failure notice that is caused by a desktop-to-mobile or mobile-to-desktop redirection that your system caused.

- Educate the whole team on the benefits of good content structure, aiming for "chunkable" content that can be reused and reorganized without needing to be rewritten.

---

[15] Get on board and find out more about being future-friendly: http://futurefriend.ly/.

Chapter 6

Responsive Boilerplate

Boilerplate is readily reusable code—a template, if you like—that you can use as a basis for your projects. Extracted from a website, the boilerplate code is what you use over and over again without changes to start off a project or a file.

Often, you'll know you're using boilerplate because it forms your first task when you start a project (usually copying and pasting from a "skeleton" into your project). A good boilerplate takes advantage of the wealth of research done by the Web community, providing optimized, best-practice baseline code. It enables you to hit the ground running, reducing your development time as you start to customize.

 What's the catch?

While boilerplates can reduce development time, they often depend on incorrect assumptions about your project's needs. This can affect their suitability for your use. For example, they may support browsers and devices irrelevant to your target audience at the cost of your site's performance. This emphasizes the need to understand the nuts and bolts of boilerplates and make informed decisions about when to use them.

There's some contention about whether boilerplate is good or not. For the purposes of this chapter, we're going to take the line that having some boilerplate code is a good way to get cracking on a project with an intelligent set of defaults.

In this chapter, we'll look at three aspects of boilerplates in responsive web design. First, we'll examine the features of a responsive boilerplate, including common goals of popular websites' boilerplates.

Secondly, we'll cover the considerations that go into designing a customized boilerplate. By knowing how to build your own custom boilerplate, you'll be able to establish a set of personalized boilerplates that are well-aligned to your common projects' requirements yet maximize code reuse; for example, one for a single client's projects based on their known target audience, one for web industry applications, one for small to medium enterprises (SMEs), and one for retrofitting complex, legacy enterprise websites. The effective use of boilerplates can help in rapidly developing new responsive websites and retrofitting existing websites to become responsive.

Finally, we'll touch on incorporating responsive boilerplates into your workflow using preprocessors, dependency managers, and build tools.

Basic Web Page Boilerplate

From a web development perspective, a basic boilerplate could look as follows:

```
<!DOCTYPE html>
<html>
<head>
  <meta charset=utf-8>
  <title></title>
</head>
<body>

</body>
</html>
```

In a single file, we have defined a valid doctype, and, while basic, have created some good semantic structure with a `title` in the `head`, and an empty `body`. We've also defined a valid character encoding for the page. This is the type of structural boilerplate almost all web developers would have committed to memory or have a shortcut in their text editor to produce.

Off-the-shelf Boilerplates

Moving on to more advanced offerings, there are many boilerplates for responsive web design in existence. You can learn a lot by picking them apart and pulling out the bits relevant to you.

HTML5 Boilerplate

HTML5 Boilerplate (H5BP), shown in Figure 6.1, is an extensively used boilerplate and actively developed project.

Figure 6.1. The H5BP home page

H5BP is aimed squarely at modern browsers by default and provides some graceful degradation options for older ones. The baseline version even provides a warning to IE7 and earlier users by telling them to upgrade their browser using a Chrome Frame.[1] If you need to target older browsers and devices, there may be better options.

Initializr[2] is a tool that produces a custom H5BP (or Bootstrap) project for you. There has been some work done to create good defaults for responsive layouts.

---

[1] http://www.google.com/chromeframe
[2] http://www.initializr.com

Mobile Boilerplate (MBP)

A spin-off of the H5BP project is HTML5 Mobile Boilerplate.[3] Just like the original H5BP where the code is aimed at providing a minimal boilerplate for desktop web projects, MBP is aimed at mobile web projects. The code isn't designed to be responsive, but it does make some mobile-specific optimizations. Notably, these include replacing jQuery with Zepto in order to be more lightweight while still being jQuery-like in most cases.

Bootstrap

Bootstrap provides a lot more functionality than HTML5 Boilerplate. Where H5BP is a minimal boilerplate (although some argue otherwise[4]) for a developer who wants a lot of control, Bootstrap takes the opposite view and includes the kitchen as well as the kitchen sink. This means that choices about font sizes, grid systems, and responsiveness are all made for you out of the box.

If you don't like default Bootstrap, you can decide what to package up using a little tool on the website.[5] As Bootstrap is built using LESS,[6] it can take the variables you provide and give you totally personalized CSS that can be used in your project, as shown in Figure 6.2.

Figure 6.2. Same HTML, new skin, minimal effort

---

[3] http://html5boilerplate.com/mobile/
[4] http://csswizardry.com/2011/01/the-real-html5-boilerplate/
[5] http://twitter.github.com/bootstrap/customize.html
[6] http://lesscss.org

Using the same HTML and modifying a couple of top-level variables on the Bootstrap site allows us to create a fully customized theme without having to use any LESS tooling.

Foundation

Foundation[7] is a responsive boilerplate made by ZURB that's designed to be responsive out of the box, leaning heavily on a grid system that adapts across different devices. The latest version takes a mobile-first approach and employs the lighter Zepto JavaScript library rather than jQuery. It is heavily geared towards rapid prototyping, encouraging design overrides and avoiding the issue Bootstrap suffers of sites looking too "Bootstrappy." While it was originally intended for prototyping, it is growing into an excellent boilerplate solution.

Skeleton

Skeleton[8] is a minimal framework geared toward cellphone-oriented displays that allow scaling out to bigger sizes. It's based on a 960-Grid-System-like approach at higher resolutions, which then stack or remove items at the lower resolutions. Skeleton is a better option for mobile-oriented sites where you may be creating an experience distinct from desktop contexts.

Semantic Grid System

The Semantic Grid System[9] project takes a different slant on the standard grid system by using the power of CSS preprocessors (support for LESS, Sass/SCSS,[10] and Stylus[11]) alongside more purely semantic HTML. The aim of the project is to do away with the conventional pattern of:

```
<article class="span4">...</article>
<aside class="span3">...</aside>
```

Here, HTML is littered with layout instructions that have little relevance when you resize responsively; for example, a small mobile device is likely to render the span3

---

[7] http://foundation.zurb.com/

[8] http://www.getskeleton.com/

[9] http://semantic.gs

[10] http://sass-lang.com/

[11] http://learnboost.github.com/stylus/

and the span4 at 100% width. Unfortunately, the project has had minimal activity of late. Still, the base is solid and worth considering if you seek clean and highly structured HTML and aim to deliver different CSS to the browser depending on the device type.

320 and up

This project was created by Andy Clarke[12] to address the need for a responsive framework that started from the position of mobile-first and progressive enhancement up to desktop, rather than degradation from desktop to mobile. The project itself takes influences from HTML5 Boilerplate, as well as Bootstrap and others. Impressively, there are bindings for the framework in LESS, Sass/SCSS, and Compass, which makes it readily usable by anyone familiar with a preprocessor.

Building Your Own Boilerplate

Any off-the-shelf solution will be based on assumptions about the project. It will be unsuitable for some particular projects, workflows, or coding styles. Let's build a customized boilerplate and look at some of the core elements of a boilerplate as we go. These include:

- folder structure
- resetting CSS
- base code and libraries: HTML structure, CSS, JS
- packaging

Folder Structure and Core Files

With so many files needed to make a good web application, having some order in your file structure helps keep your projects logical and maintainable. The usual approach is to have the minimal amount in the root directory, and place everything else into logical directories, as shown in Figure 6.3.

---

[12] http://stuffandnonsense.co.uk/projects/320andup/

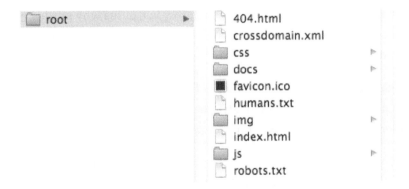

Figure 6.3. Keep your root folder clean

The reason to clear out the clutter is because your root folder tends to be a jumping-off point into your project, and needs to contain a wide range of files and metadata such as:

- index file
- **robots.txt** file
- favicon files
- various touch icons for iOS
- some server-side files, such as **.htaccess** or other config-related files
- version control files such as **.gitignore**
- **crossdomain.xml** file if you need to enable cross-domain access for technologies such as Flash and Silverlight (or the other libraries that use it)

Good practice would also see you include the following:

- **humans.txt** file to provide info about the team that worked on the project
- project **readme** file
- **LICENSE** file, especially if you're working on an open-source project.
- **CONTRIBUTING** file for how developers can contribute to your open-source project
- requirements file, such as a **requirements.txt, Gemfile**, or **package.json** file[13]

---

[13] This is common in frameworks where a package manager is used to install dependencies, such as Python's PyPI (the Python Package Index) [http://pypi.python.org/pypi], Ruby's RubyGems [http://rubygems.org/], or Node's NPM [https://npmjs.org/].

That's a lot of files we should have in the root, so you can see why putting everything else into nicely organized directories can help. Typically, the minimum these directories comprise are:

- an images folder (called **img**, **images**, or **i**)
- a CSS folder (called **css**, **styles**, or **stylesheets**)
- a JavaScript folder (called **js**, **scripts**, or **javascripts**)

In addition, you may want to consider other structures depending on your framework and libraries. For example, you might distinguish between static or structural files—used to make your core site work (such as logos)—and media files, which are images or other rich content uploaded via a CMS or by users. Making this type of distinction keeps your assets management clean, tidy, and much more maintainable.

WDS Folder Structure and Files

Let's see this in action. Continuing with our Web Directions South example, we've elected to use condensed folder names to keep our URL paths short (shaving bytes everywhere!):

- **img** for all our image assets
- **css** for our stylesheets
- **js** for our script files
- **lib** for our third-party JavaScript libraries

For our core files, let's mix and match some favorites, and build our **index.html** file as we go. From 320 and Up, we'll grab the default **robots.txt** file:

```
                                            chapter06/boilerplate/robots.txt
# www.robotstxt.org/
# http://code.google.com/web/controlcrawlindex/

User-agent: *
```

... and **humans.txt**:

```
/* humanstxt.org */

/* TEAM */

Name:      eg: Andy Clarke
Site:      eg: http://stuffandnonsense.co.uk
Twitter:   eg: @malarkey
Location:  eg: UK

/* THANKS */

Conor MacNeill (http://twitter.com/thefella) for the responsive type
➡ PHP port.
https://github.com/thefella/Responsive-type-references

Lennart Schoors (http://twitter.com/lensco) for the responsive desig
➡n test page
https://gist.github.com/1685127

/* SITE */

Standards:

HTML5
CSS3

Components:

320 and Up:   http://stuffandnonsense.co.uk/projects/320andup
⋮
```

If these robots and humans files are new to you, the examples also show you websites from which to find more information.

To deliver favicons successfully to a range of devices and produce beautiful and functional cellphone home-screen icons, you need the right combination of link attributes and image assets of assorted sizes. From H5BP, we'll grab its **favicon.ico** and its suggested selection of touch icon files. These indicate the different versions of the favicon file you need to supply. Which favicon files you supply and how you link to them is tied strongly to the level of browser and device support you're offering. We have settled for a reasonably backwards-compatible combination of link elements and attributes, but it's advisable to investigate this area further yourself. We'll combine two robust favicon approaches[14] for a solution bordering on overkill and add the following `link` elements to our **index.html**:

chapter06/boilerplate/index.html *(excerpt)*

```html
<!-- http://mathiasbynens.be/notes/touch-icons -->
<!-- For third-generation iPad with high-resolution Retina
  display: -->
<link rel="apple-touch-icon-precomposed" sizes="144x144"
  href="apple-touch-icon-144x144-precomposed.png">

<!-- For iPhone with high-resolution Retina display: -->
<link rel="apple-touch-icon-precomposed" sizes="114x114"
  href="apple-touch-icon-114x114-precomposed.png">

<!-- For first- and second-generation iPad: -->
<link rel="apple-touch-icon-precomposed" sizes="72x72"
  href="apple-touch-icon-72x72-precomposed.png">

<!-- For non-Retina iPhone, iPod Touch, and Android 2.1+
  devices: -->
<link rel="apple-touch-icon-precomposed"
  href="apple-touch-icon-precomposed.png">

<!-- http://www.jonathantneal.com/blog/understand-the-favicon/ -->
<link rel="icon" href="favicon.png">
<!--[if IE]>
  <link rel="shortcut icon" href="favicon.ico">
<![endif]-->
<!-- or, set /favicon.ico for IE10 win -->
<meta name="msapplication-TileColor" content="#D83434">
<meta name="msapplication-TileImage" content="tileicon.png">
```

This should support the various Apple devices, Android devices, IE6+, and modern browsers. Here, we've included the commented sources for our design decision, as well as instructive comments (for example, `<!-- or, set /favicon.ico for IE10 win -->`). Including comments this way in your boilerplate can serve as a reminder further down the track for why you made that decision. As technology changes and

---

[14] http://mathiasbynens.be/notes/touch-icons and
http://www.jonathantneal.com/blog/understand-the-favicon/

your support for older devices drops off, they'll serve as flags for components of your boilerplate that need updating.

We'll take some notes from H5BP and drop in **404.html**, **.gitignore**, and **crossdomain.xml** files as reminders of development aspects on which we need to make decisions. Finally, for the same reason, we'll drop in some empty **CONTRIBUTING.md**, **LICENSE.md**, and **README.md** files.

Resetting and Normalizing

CSS resets are stylesheets developed to address the inconsistencies between default styles of HTML elements across browsers. They operate by essentially removing all default browser styles on elements that have distinct defaults in different browsers.

Similarly, **normalizing CSS files** are used to rectify the inconsistencies between browsers. Instead of setting everything back to zero as in the case of resets, however, normalizing CSS files maintain many useful browser defaults and aim to bring them to a consistent state.

Having a solid CSS reset, or CSS normalization, allows you to start from a known, consistent baseline; for example, you can rely on all browsers to render your web page with the same page margin and padding. Given the advancing standards by browser vendors, the days of resetting every box-model property to zero are quickly disappearing, but there are still some quirks between browsers that need ironing out.

There are plenty of choices, from the venerable "Meyerweb Reset" that sets everything back to zero,[15] through to normalize.css.[16] It's used in projects such as Bootstrap and H5BP, and is more about consistency across browsers. If you want to explore a range of reset options, a good list can be found at CSS Reset.[17]

Generally, start with one of the standard resetting options and then apply your own additions to them if needed. Use caution when you are resetting styles to a zero position (or normalizing them to a consistent state) to avoid providing real styling, such as using your brand's fonts and colors. If you've crossed this line, you probably

---

[15] http://meyerweb.com/eric/tools/css/reset/

[16] http://necolas.github.com/normalize.css/

[17] http://www.cssreset.com/

want to start moving these rules to a base CSS file instead, which we'll see in the section called "Base CSS".

WDS Resets

For our example, we'll reuse the **reset.css** file introduced in the section called "Media Queries in Action" in Chapter 4 and update our **index.html** links:

chapter06/boilerplate/index.html *(excerpt)*

```
<link rel="stylesheet" href="css/reset.css">
```

Base Libraries

A good baseline goes beyond reducing browser differences to ensuring correct positioning of items, introducing placeholders for common tasks, hooks for detecting device features, and more. In addition to a CSS reset, for example, you might include a **base.css** file in your project to establish styles for core page components across the entire site. A base could include some structural HTML, site-wide CSS, and JavaScript.

Structural HTML

Depending on your philosophy, having some basic HTML structure provided by your boilerplate can be useful. For example, H5BP has some basic HTML structure out of the box, which is mostly about enforcing good practices around where to place elements in a page to minimize bugs and improve performance.[18] On the other hand, a lot of HTML in your boilerplate code is probably overkill. That navigation bar would be wasted on your one-page app, although you might consider a compromise:

chapter06/boilerplate/index.html *(excerpt)*

```
<!DOCTYPE html>
<!--[if lt IE 7]>
  <html class="no-js lt-ie9 lt-ie8 lt-ie7" lang="en">
<![endif]-->
<!--[if (IE 7)&!(IEMobile)]>
  <html class="no-js lt-ie9 lt-ie8" lang="en">
```

---

[18] http://www.phpied.com/conditional-comments-block-downloads/

```
<![endif]-->
<!--[if (IE 8)&!(IEMobile)]>
  <html class="no-js lt-ie9" lang="en">
<![endif]-->
<!--[if gt IE 8]>
  <!--> <html class="no-js" lang="en"><!--
<![endif]-->
  <head>
    <meta charset=utf-8>
    <meta name=viewport
      content="width=device-width, initial-scale=1.0">
    <title>…</title>
    <link rel="stylesheet" href="css/style.css">
    <link rel="stylesheet" href="css/tablet.css"
      media="all and (min-width: 480px)">
    <link rel="stylesheet" href="css/desktop.css"
      media="all and (min-width: 960px)">
    <script src="js/modernizr-2.5.3-min.js"></script>
    ⋮
    <link rel="icon" href="favicon.png">
    ⋮
  </head>
  <body>
    <header>
      <!-- main header stuff in here -->
    </header>
    <section class="container">
      <h1>Page title</h1>
      <!-- main page content in here -->
    </section>
    <footer>
      <!-- footer elements -->
    </footer>
    <script src="//ajax.googleapis.com/ajax/libs/jquery/1.7.2/jquery
➡.min.js"></script>
    <script>window.jQuery || document.write('<script src="js/jquery-
➡1.7.2.min.js"><\/script>')</script>
  </body>
</html>
```

This fairly minimal boilerplate has taken approaches from many sources, including H5BP and Modernizr. Taking a mobile-first approach, the hooks for IE detection include media queries for !(IEMobile). This boilerplate also provides a baseline with correct positioning of items, some placeholders for common tasks, and reminders to fill in the basics including required CSS and JavaScript libraries, as well as header, main content, and footer elements.

Base CSS

Your base CSS should contain all of your site-wide branding and style decisions. For a responsive site, you may want to include the grid system in this file. Choosing a grid system will vary depending on the markup required of the grid system, and whether you're retrofitting an existing site or starting from scratch. As an example, migrating nonsemantic legacy HTML to a grid system that's heavily dependent on layout-based classes (.span4 and friends) could be a bad idea.

Furthermore, if your responsive website takes a mobile-first approach, the base CSS file will sometimes contain the smaller device-specific styles. Take care to avoid asking too much of your base file, though, as overloading it could lead to inheritance nightmares. You might, instead, take a modular, object-oriented stance to writing CSS.

Unfortunately, separating your files out as we have increases the number of network requests made to render your web page. This is where a CSS preprocessor can help out, which we will look at further in the section called "CSS Preprocessors":

```
<link rel="stylesheet" href="css/style.css">
<link rel="stylesheet" href="css/tablet.css"
  media="all and (min-width: 480px)">
<link rel="stylesheet" href="css/desktop.css"
  media="all and (min-width: 960px)">
<script src="js/modernizr-2.5.3-min.js"></script>
```

You might have noticed the script tag thrown in with the CSS there. Modernizr is an example of a JavaScript library designed to progressively enhance websites using feature detection. While it is a little weighty, it's an extremely useful library to use when you're developing with quite new HTML5 features, such as using the touch or Device APIs. As it primarily concerns style, it is front-loaded in the HTML document to avoid a flash of unstyled content (FOUC),[19] rather than deferred to the end as script tags often are for performance reasons.

---

[19] http://en.wikipedia.org/wiki/Flash_of_unstyled_content

JavaScript

Most developers will have a preference for a set of libraries that they use by default. The most common are JavaScript libraries such as jQuery, Zepto, YUI,[20] MooTools,[21] and Prototype.[22] A developer or team may be working on a single library almost exclusively, so they'll have extremely good domain knowledge in the area the library is being used. In this way, we can leverage their skill to help us. In most cases, the popular libraries used are well-maintained, so we can keep updating as improvements come along. Due to lots of people using the library, any bugs will be seen quickly and resolved rapidly: with enough eyeballs all bugs are shallow.[23]

Libraries may not be applicable in every instance, however; for example, do you need the entire jQuery library to bind some event handlers to some links?

When you are working with third-party libraries in your boilerplate, you should always look to use the latest versions in order to reap the benefits of patches to known bugs, as well as enjoy the latest features. This may, however, require work to update your boilerplate. If you're spending too much time adapting your boilerplate for each project, you need to refine your processes. We'll look at packaging and production in the section called "Packaging for Reuse".

Packaging for Reuse

Your first task when establishing your boilerplate is to look at your process. When you start a project, what are you doing in the first instance every time? You might set up a directory structure, or copy and paste certain files. A good way to document this is by using a version control system: start a new project and commit each step you take that's not to do with project-specific code. You can tag particular points to help you find the non-project-specific code later for reusing and building your boilerplate. Examining your process helps you establish a pattern of tasks you perform time and again.

---

[20] http://yuilibrary.com/
[21] http://mootools.net/
[22] http://prototypejs.org/
[23] http://en.wikipedia.org/wiki/Linus's_Law

Once you have a good view of your process, you can then look at steps to automate production, such as bundling all the code together into a project skeleton, or doing some scripting to produce the code you need.

CSS Preprocessors

Preprocessing is a form of meta-programming. Using preprocessors for CSS makes a lot of sense, though it will alter your workflow. Instead of working in normal CSS, you work in an intermediate file format and syntax, which you then compile. Compilation may be performed server-side with a command-line tool or GUI, or client-side by the browser (although that's inadvisable for production) to turn the intermediary into regular CSS. For modern CSS, this can speed up your development enormously.

Popular preprocessors like Sass/SCSS and LESS[24] can handle tasks such as allowing you to define all the vendor prefixes of a particular CSS attribute, so that you only need to use them once in your code, reducing significant clutter in your source files. Often, you can do jobs like nesting (so that your CSS matches your DOM structure) and many other useful time-savers, such as function calls and mixins.

Taking CSS preprocessing one step further, these preprocessors can be used to watch folders and trigger automatic compilation of preprocessed files. You can use them to version your CSS files, assisting in development and caching. To improve site performance and therefore user experience, CSS preprocessor apps can be used to combine and minify your output CSS files, yet preserve your modular and maintainable source files. Let's see some of these bonuses.

WDS CSS Preprocessing

The Sass home page includes Ruby instructions to kick off your Sass adventure:

```
$ gem install sass
$ mv style.css style.scss
$ sass --watch style.scss:style.css
```

---

[24] We'll skip providing an opinion on Sass vs LESS here, as it's a bit like the Chrome vs Firefox or Emacs vs Vim debate. For a good explanation on why Twitter decided to use LESS, check out its post on the matter: http://www.wordsbyf.at/2012/03/08/why-less/ I'd definitely recommend trying both out, though.

This installs Sass, turns your **.css** file into a **.scss** file, and watches the Sass file for changes. If the Sass file is updated, it automatically compiles and updates your CSS file. To learn more about installing and using a CSS preprocessor, check out the respective preprocessor's website. For now, let's see what we can do with our boilerplate. Here we've converted our CSS file to SCSS:

chapter06/boilerplate/css/base.scss *(excerpt)*

```
#content div.speaker img {
  border-radius: 45px;
  width: 90px;
}

@media only screen and (-webkit-min-device-pixel-ratio: 2) {
  #content div.speaker img {
    border-radius: 90px;
    width: 180px;
  }
}
```

What can we do about the repetition? Let's give Sass variables and mixins a spin. Firstly, we declare some variables using dollar signs ($avatar-radius and $scale) at the top of the file so they're easy to find:

chapter06/boilerplate/css/base.scss *(excerpt)*

```
$avatar-radius: 45px;
$scale: 1;
```

Next, we'll employ those variables and some arithmetic:

chapter06/boilerplate/css/base.scss *(excerpt)*

```
#content div.speaker img {
  border-radius: $avatar-radius;
  width: $avatar-radius*2;
}
```

As the width is exactly double the border-radius for our speaker avatar img, we use our original $avatar-radius of 45px times two to calculate the desired width of 90px.

If you're following along, check that the CSS output from your Sass still reflects your original style declarations. Now we want to reuse the border-radius and width declarations so let's move those into a mixin:

chapter06/boilerplate/css/base.scss *(excerpt)*

```scss
@mixin avatar {
  border-radius: $avatar-radius;
  width: $avatar-radius*2;
}

#content div.speaker img {
  @include avatar;
}
```

Here, we use an @include to pull our new mixin called avatar into our speaker avatar style declaration.

Finally, we can supply a parameter to our mixin using parentheses:

chapter06/boilerplate/css/base.scss *(excerpt)*

```scss
@mixin avatar($scale) {
  border-radius: $avatar-radius*$scale;
  width: $avatar-radius*2*$scale;
}

#content div.speaker img {
  @include avatar(1);
}

@media only screen and (-webkit-min-device-pixel-ratio: 2) {
  #content div.speaker img {
    @include avatar(2);
  }
}
```

This takes the $scale variable we declared previously and supplies that to the mixin as a parameter when we pull it into our styles using @include(). Now we can programmatically double the border-radius and width for -webkit- devices with a higher pixel density.

We only need to declare our speaker image styles once and update the variable values for different device contexts. This way, we ensure we're sticking to the DRY (Don't Repeat Yourself) principle, saving ourselves time and improving the modularity of our code.

By continuing abstracting code away like this, we would eventually reach a state where we could comfortably add new breakpoints with our media queries, set variables declaring our new targeted screen sizes, and the new styles would be easily generated. This would allow us to fine-tune our breakpoints without increasing the resources required to maintain the multiple layouts.

Script Management

Another consideration is the role of third-party dependencies in your boilerplate. For example, H5BP comes packaged with Modernizr. Similarly, jQuery is commonly required to use certain libraries, so if you have more than one of these in your system, you may end up with multiple downloads of jQuery.

Do you want to always use the latest version, or use a particular version until you decide to update officially? Moving to the latest version of a project that your code depends on may require time-consuming activities such as examining change logs, performing manual tests, and updating your project to maintain compatibility. While you may gain more features and stability by using the latest release, version breaks can be a hassle.

With these factors in mind, you may consider picking up a dedicated JavaScript package manager such as Ender[25] or Jam.[26] Imagine if you wanted to use all the excellent microframeworks at Microjs[27]—they could save you some trouble. Further, Bower[28] is a useful browser package manager that handles front-end dependencies, including image assets, CSS, and JavaScript, so you no longer need to manually download or manage your scripts or CSS libraries. You should also consider automating your processes with a task runner such as Grunt.[29]

---

[25] https://github.com/ender-js/Ender

[26] http://jamjs.org/

[27] http://microjs.com

[28] http://twitter.github.com/bower/

[29] http://gruntjs.com/

If you want to always update to the latest versions of such upstream projects, consider using submodules or some metaprogramming to install them in your projects.

Ship It

Once you have your boilerplate code together, how do you package it up for reuse? You could just keep it in a folder on your desktop, but you should consider keeping it in a version-controlled repository (such as Git). If your code is free of commercially sensitive information, you could even consider releasing it as open source for others to use as well. If this is your first time releasing your code to the masses, you need to understand the differences between licences (TLDRLegal[30] is a good starting point). This book's code archive, including our new boilerplate, is in a Git repository.

When You Boil It Down ...

Boilerplate code provides a speedy way of giving you a good baseline set of code to use to build your application. The purpose of a boilerplate is to give you a starting point of common standards that work across asset handling, CSS, JavaScript, and your HTML structure. The key points from this chapter are:

- By developing your own boilerplate, you can be sure that it suits your own projects and coding style, contains no redundant code, and you know exactly what it does—absolutely no more than it needs to.

- If you build your own boilerplate, it should be giving you an advantage in standards, time-saving, and stability. If you're spending too much time adapting your boilerplate for each project, you need to refine it.

- Preprocessing may provide better boilerplate code if you're setting up target templates or projects using template routing.

- There are many good boilerplates out there, so do what many have done before you and start with one of these—get a feel for what it can (and can't) do.

- There's no need to stick to an off-the-shelf solution. If your intentions differ from another developer's, it doesn't mean you're wrong; you might just have a different use case.

---

[30] http://www.tldrlegal.com/

Respond in Kind

Responsive web design is more than just a methodology that strives to help you focus on your users by providing a collection of best practices. Sure it *is* a collection of best practices, but they're practices that strive to stay out of sight and let you make decisions as quickly as possible. They're practices that bolster your design, rather than box it in.

Where other Web movements are focused on creators, RWD is focused on your creation—your users can see the benefits because they can access your application more easily. Where other Web movements are concerned with curly braces and semi-colons, RWD deals with the very practical issue of the explosion of devices from which your users access your application.

More than just fluid grids, adaptive images, media queries, and dynamic content, responsive web design is the jetpack that flies your users to the future of design.

Lightning Source UK Ltd.
Milton Keynes UK
UKOW06f1358130914

238426UK00002BA/80/P